In Role:

Teaching and Learning Dramatically

PATRICK VERRIOUR

Pippin Publishing Limited

Acknowledgment

Grateful acknowledgment is made for permission to reprint the poems on page 36 from *Prints in the Sand*, an anthology of poems by British Columbia students submitted to "Pandora's Box." Edited by Sydney Butler and Norma Jamieson, Vancouver: British Columbia English Teachers' Association, 1978.

Designed by John Zehethofer
Edited by Sylvia Hill
Typeset by Jay Tee Graphics Ltd.
Printed and bound by Kromar Printing Ltd.

Canadian Cataloguing in Publication Data

Verriour, Patrick
  In role: teaching and learning dramatically

(The Pippin teacher's library ; 14)
Includes bibliographical references.
ISBN 0-88751-058-2

1. Role playing. 2. Teaching. 3. Interdisciplinary approach in education. I. Title. II. Series.

LB1027.B47 1993   371.3'32   C93-093985-9

CONTENTS

. . . .

INTRODUCTION

Man only plays when he is in the full sense of the word a Human Being, and
he is only fully human when he is at play.

Friedrich Schiller

A colleague of mine in visual arts education is studying ways in which elementary teachers develop their classroom
art programs. Through her discussions with individual teachers,
she has discovered that they do not perceive any differences
between their teaching of art and other subject areas in the curriculum. For these teachers, children's education is viewed as
a holistic, integrated learning experience rather than one that
seeks to compartmentalize learning into discrete disciplines often
isolated from one another.

I have written this book in the firm belief that bridges should
be built between the arts and other areas of the curriculum if
children are to discover fresh perspectives in their understanding of the world in which they live, and different ways of expressing their thoughts and ideas. Above all, the arts have a special
role to play in human learning because they celebrate what we
share in common, while at the same time recognizing and
respecting our unique cultural differences.

For a number of years, I have been involved in demonstrat-
ing ways in which classroom drama can be used as a medium
for integrating learning across the curriculum. Yet, as I have discovered after teaching drama in education courses at both under-
graduate and graduate levels and after giving countless
workshops, the use of drama as a medium of learning still
remains relatively unknown to many teachers, while others do
not feel they have the necessary background or expertise to use
drama in their teaching.

The main purpose of this book, therefore, is to make drama
accessible to those elementary teachers who are already seeking fresh ways to give purpose and meaning to their students'

learning. For many years, teachers of younger students have been in the vanguard of educational change. Their creative and innovative classrooms and integrated curricula bear testimony to this. These teachers know the value of play in children's lives and in their education. I hope that through this book they will also come to appreciate how dramatic playing can enrich the learning in their classrooms.

Over the years the writing and teaching of Gavin Bolton, David Booth, Dorothy Heathcote, Norah Morgan, Cecily O'Neill, Juliana Saxton and Carole Tarlington have influenced my work profoundly. I value their friendship, and the generosity with which they have shared their considerable talents.

I would like to thank all those teachers and students whose continued work in the field of drama in education have provided me with the stimulus for writing this book. In particular, I would like to thank Heather Bazeluk for permission to use her material for drama teaching in *Playing Dramatically*, and Vicki Jensen for the material related to Sir John Franklin. Both teachers attended courses I taught and it is a great pleasure for me to use their work as exemplary models of dramatic playing. I would also like to thank Sally Clinton and Lee Gunderson for their support. Finally, one primary teacher, my wife Angela, has given me many insights into young children's dramatic playing, and I am grateful to her for her advice and support.

. . . .

PLAYING DRAMATICALLY

Integrating Learning in Drama

Watching children working in drama provides fascinating insights into the richness of their imaginations, the skill with which they negotiate with one another, their present level of critical thinking, and the sophistication of the language they use. To give you some sense of the range of learning experiences that can occur when students are engaged in classroom drama, here are some snapshot pictures of children about eleven years of age in Richmond, British Columbia, tackling some tough issues in their drama work.

The students have been studying European medieval castles as part of their social studies program. In drama, they have decided to find out what it would be like to live in a castle and train to be a squire. Working with their teacher, they have created a training school for squires that is located in the castle. Both boys and girls are in the role of squires, and the teacher is in role as the master of arms who instructs them in their obligations and duties.

Before they complete their training, the master of arms receives a message from the lord of the castle telling him the lord urgently needs young squires willing to accompany him on a Crusade. The young squires talk about the decision facing them and what it may mean to them. Some are full of bravado, eager to go, while others are less certain about the prospect. Writing in role, all of them discuss their personal feelings in their daily journals.

One young squire, Jennifer, voices her misgivings and fears about being selected to go. In role as squire, she writes:

> Tomorrow we will find out who is chosen and I am praying that I'm not chosen. I get sick from the sight of blood. I can't

even stand using a weapon. I was sent by my father against my will but I never dared to tell him that. I just want to take care of horses and some day become a great rider. I also don't want to be chosen because I got word that my dear sister Marie is very ill and I want to take care of her. But if I am chosen I must go.

Now the squires are divided by the master of arms into two groups: those that want to go, and those who are unwilling to bear arms. Suddenly, the proceedings are interrupted by another of squire Jennifer's sisters with a message from her parents insisting that she go on the Crusade to uphold the family name and honor. But, of course, Jennifer has already made up her mind that she does not want to go. Now all of the squires are asked to consider whether or not Jennifer should volunteer, and obey her parents, or stand by her original decision and refuse to go.

Weighing up the pros and cons of the situation, one student in role as squire writes:

> I feel Jennifer of Leung should go talk to his family, and tell them his feelings, and if his family still feels as strongly, he should ask Sir Geoffrey if he is skilled enough and if he says yes, he should go on the Crusade and just train until he goes. If he chooses not to go he should keep training, and go on another one.

Is this drama or is it social studies or is it something else? Here is what some of the children in the class had to say about what they had learned during this drama — when they talked to one of my graduate students, Sabina Harpe,[1] who was collecting data for her thesis:

> ... when we were doing drama it combined with science and our castle work 'cause we learned about different ways like friction and things like that so it also helps with Science too and things like that ...

> ... writing I think is the main thing in drama. Science can be involved in it and also Social Studies 'cause castles is our Social Studies and with that we're writing about doing Social Studies too so that combines with lots of different work and Mathematical problems go along with science.

> ... what do you mean by learning because we're learning *in*

drama like we're doing stuff. O.K., we're doing castles and then we started drama with castle squires, so we have to pretend we're squires now and I think we can learn from it because we read books and do work and watch movies about castle life and now we're going to act.

One can almost hear the note of exasperation in the last student's voice at being asked to explain something that seems perfectly obvious to her. For the children in this class, their work in drama enables them to integrate knowledge they have acquired in new and interesting ways so that they gain fresh insights into the world in which they live. Their teacher has emphasized the importance of drama as a powerful medium of learning by providing a central role for it in her classroom curriculum.

Dramatic Playing

The form of drama in which this class is involved is different from the rehearsed, scripted performances we are used to seeing performed by actors for an audience in the commercial or amateur theater. Implicit within this concept of theater (called *dramatic playing* by the British drama educator Gavin Bolton) is the assumption that the entire classroom space in which the activity occurs is the stage or playing area, and the participants, who are engaged in creating the dramatic context, perform for one another.

Dramatic playing, therefore, is characterized by a high degree of spontaneity as teacher and students work to create a fictional world in which they assume roles to explore issues that are of concern to them. The central purpose of dramatic playing is to contextualize learning in such a way that it has purpose and meaning for students and enables them, through reflection, to reach new levels of thinking and understanding in their intellectual, emotional, social, and language development. Because they are engaged in learning through the use of the dramatic art form, dramatic playing also enhances their understanding of the power of drama in their lives.

In this book, I describe some of the ways in which dramatic playing can make significant contributions to student learning across and beyond the curriculum, and I provide practical suggestions of how and when you, the teacher, can use drama. I also examine how drama can help students identify with the challenges human beings face in their lives at a very personal level, and I emphasize the importance of regarding drama as a social encounter in which the participants work together to create dramatic contexts.

Areas of Learning

To give some sense of the variety and breadth of learning dimensions that can occur in a dramatic context which faces students with tough issues and decisions, let's take a second look at the medieval drama outlined above from a number of different perspectives.

In order to clarify the different sorts of learning that were occurring in the medieval drama, I group them under five areas of learning: intellectual, emotional, social, drama (aesthetic), and language. All categories have equal value when it comes to learning in drama; my ordering them in this way does not imply that weight and emphasis is being given to one dimension over another.

INTELLECTUAL

This area of learning involves students' changes in understanding about the human themes, concepts, and values that may be encountered in a specific dramatic context. For example, in addition to using the knowledge and concepts that they may have acquired in a particular subject area, students are required to apply their learning to grapple with a problem contained in the dramatic context. For instance, a student might ask: What do I now know and what do I need to know in order to serve the lord of the castle on the Crusade?

In order to create and maintain a dramatic context, students not only develop an awareness of what they know, they also discover gaps in their existing knowledge and understanding. This requires them to think critically, ask questions, and undertake further research. They now acquire new knowledge, which should assist them in shedding a clearer light on their understanding of a topic or issue.

Key elements of the intellectual area of learning in drama include:

— Recalling past experiences, thoughts, ideas, relevant information, and images.

- Thinking through a sequence of events.
- Making informed choices and decisions.
- Seeing the implications and consequences of one's choices and actions.
- Being aware of similarities and differences.
- Seeing relationships.
- Seeing alternatives.
- Thinking metaphorically and allegorically.
- Focusing and clarifying images.
- Making judgments.
- Thinking hypothetically.
- Thinking intuitively.

EMOTIONAL

I have already referred in passing to the students' own knowledge that they bring to the drama. This knowledge along with personal feelings, attitudes, values, and beliefs constitutes a crucial element in any drama.

In the medieval drama, the students in role as squires respond in their journals individually at a number of different levels to the proposition that they should accompany the lord on the Crusade. Jennifer, the squire who will later be chosen to go, reveals in her writing her role's *attitude* (her decision to become a squire was made against all her personal wishes at the instigation of her father whom she obeyed), her *emotions* and *feelings* (she is concerned about her sister who is ill), her *physical* response (she admits she is sickened by the sight of blood), and a certain element of *spirituality* (she prays that she will not be chosen).

Through her writing, Jennifer is able to clarify the values, attitudes, and feelings of the role she is taking before the actual decision to send her is made. A quick survey of other students' journals revealed that most of them felt that Jennifer should go and not disgrace her father. However, in her role as unwilling squire, Jennifer sustains the integrity of playing someone who has been forced into a way of life or career against her wishes, and who knows when to stand her ground to defend her principles.

The truth and authenticity with which each individual in role responds to the dramatic situation is crucial to the success of the dramatic learning experience for all participants.

Key elements in the emotional area of learning in drama include:

— Recalling past emotions and feelings.
— Expressing emotions and feelings.
— Understanding emotions.
— Identifying with the emotions and feelings of others.
— Formulating and being aware of personal beliefs, values, and attitudes.
— Expressing emotions, personal beliefs, values, and attitudes, which may be different to their own.
— Valuing themselves and feeling a sense of self worth.
— Feeling they are empowered to act and make changes.

SOCIAL

Social learning is inherent in the collaborative nature of the work itself. Without an initial contract or agreement being made between the teacher and all participants to explore what it is like to live in a medieval castle, the dramatic playing cannot begin.

Therefore, the social interactions or negotiations that occur in class discussions *about* the dramatic context are as important as those that occur *within* the imaginary or "as if" situation. Both are crucial to the creation and maintenance of an imaginary context. At the same time, there is another important aspect of social learning that should not be ignored, and this involves the learning about others that occurs within the drama itself.

In the medieval castle drama, the students are not only asked to decide how their roles would respond to the lord's summons, they are also asked to comment on squire Jennifer's decision not to go. As squires, the students are placed in a situation where they are required to consider another perspective or point of view, and give advice to squire Jennifer about her personal dilemma.

Key elements in the social area of learning in drama include:

— Accepting the ideas of others.
— Sharing their ideas with others.
— Tolerating differences in others.
— Being aware of and respecting other points of view.
— Taking a contrary point of view.
— Taking and expressing a point of view, which may well be different from their own.

— Understanding how a group functions.
— Taking a leadership role when necessary.
— Assuming a subordinate role when necessary.
— Playing a mediating role when necessary.
— Going along with and abiding by group decisions.
— Knowing how to work with others.
— Knowing how to work alone alongside others.

DRAMA (AESTHETIC)

Learning about drama provides the clay that binds the dramatic playing, enabling the participants to shape their work in such a way that they will experience a sense of success and satisfaction in the dramatic representation of their ideas. Christopher Havel[2] describes the crucial role the teacher plays in developing the aesthetic consciousness of the students. He writes: "Unfortunately, this learning dimension is often neglected by teachers to such an extent that the dramatic elements of tension, surprise, contrast, focus, and symbolization are rarely considered."

In the medieval castle drama, one can sense the rising tension as the decision has to be made about who will accompany the lord on the Crusade (tension of enduring a test or challenge). At the same time, the sudden unannounced arrival of Jennifer's sister provides an added element of tension and surprise in the drama that not only affects the drama itself, but also the learning that occurs within the drama (tension of facing conflicting priorities).

Even very young children appear to have an instinctive and intuitive understanding and appreciation of those dramatic elements that strengthen and enrich their spontaneous make-believe play. In dramatic playing, students' growing awareness of how to manipulate the elements of drama increases their understanding of the ways in which drama works, and assists them in their exploration of the issues and themes that arise within the dramatic context.

One other aspect of drama learning that is frequently forgotten in classroom drama work is the learning associated with reflection. In the medieval drama, the journal writing gave students an opportunity to think about issues and events in the drama, and discuss them reflectively before the action of the drama moved on.

However, reflective moments may happen at any time, both

within the dramatic context itself and during moments of discussion outside the drama. Sometimes, insights gained from reflection occur days, even weeks after a drama is long over. For example, this class may be reading a book in which a character is required to make a difficult decision. It's quite possible that a student would say: "This is just like the time when squire Jennifer had to stand up to her family."

Key elements in the dramatic area of learning include:

— Tolerating ambiguity.
— Working with contrasts.
— Understanding the significance of sign and symbol.
— Understanding the importance of reflective thinking.
— Taking risks.
— Understanding the use of tension.
— Appreciating and understanding the use of ritual.
— Knowing how to vary pace and tempo.
— Being aware of the use of space, light, and sound.

LANGUAGE

It goes without saying that language is central to drama. In recent years, the argument that drama is also an integral component of children's language education has frequently been advanced by both drama and language arts educators. Special emphasis has been placed on the creation of drama learning contexts in order to provide children with the opportunity to increase their use and awareness of language.

The language of drama encompasses the different modes of expression that human beings use to communicate with one another, and encourages students to become more aware of, and sensitive to, language.

In the medieval drama, the most obvious example of language usage is the students' own writing. Because the students write in role as squires, the writing itself forces them to adopt a point of view that may not necessarily be their own. Faced with the dilemma of whether or not they should volunteer for the Crusade, many write with passion and sincerity in response to the tense dramatic situation.

Because the writing is integrated within the dramatic context, the students are provided with a purpose and an audience for their writing. In this case, as this is a journal or diary entry, they are writing for themselves, but on other occasions they write home to an imaginary family, to the lord, and to each other in their roles as squires.

In addition to the writing, there are the negotiations that occur between teacher and students, as well as between students both within and outside the dramatic context. There are the different styles or registers of language, and the special vocabulary required to give the medieval drama a sense of authenticity for the participants. There are also the physical movements and gestures which heighten and enrich the students' communication with one another, and which had a unique meaning in the age of medieval chivalry.

Quite obviously language and language learning have a very special place in drama, which the teacher using dramatic playing must learn to recognize and respond.

Key elements of the language learning area in drama include:

— Using descriptive language.
— Comparing and contrasting.
— Making predictions.
— Asking questions.
— Drawing conclusions.
— Giving opinions or ratings.
— Formulating, testing, and establishing hypotheses.
— Assessing causes and effects, motives, methods, consequences and implications.
— Developing generalizations.
— Using a variety of language styles and registers.
— Signalling intentions, and reading and responding to the signals of others.
— Questioning assumptions.
— Stating alternatives.

Drama in the Curriculum

Whenever I conduct workshops with teachers, they invariably ask me: "When and where should I use drama in the curriculum?" Because I feel drama can play a central role in students' learning, I usually encourage them to set aside a time for drama each day as a means of reflecting, synthesizing, and clarifying those issues and concerns that may have been raised in other subject areas (as in the case of the medieval drama). There will be other topics, of course, that arise out of students' everyday personal concerns, interests, and experiences that can also be explored through dramatic playing.

Realistically, I also realise that because there are so many curricular demands on a teacher's time, a subject such as drama often gives way to apparently more pressing needs such as completing a project or piece of writing in another subject area. In this book, therefore, I am concerned exclusively with describing ways in which drama can be used to enhance children's learning in two distinct although not separate ways:

1. As a central teaching and learning component in an integrated, thematic unit.
2. As a means of enhancing specific areas of learning within an integrated unit.

This does not preclude using the book for the purposes of establishing a separate drama program in the elementary classroom, but in view of the trend towards an integrated curriculum in many schools, I hope to demonstrate that it is possible to use drama in such a way that children not only learn *about* drama but also learn *through* drama.

Each of the following chapters is devoted to one aspect of the process of helping you and your class engage in dramatic playing so that your students gain fresh insights and new understandings about the concepts they are studying.

Integrating Learning Dramatically describes the links between children's spontaneous play and dramatic playing. This chapter emphasizes the importance of cooperative learning in the creation of a dramatic context; it focuses on the planning and implementation of an integrated thematic unit dealing with the theme "Working Together as a Community."

Planning Dramatically takes a closer look at teacher planning for dramatic playing in terms of the ways the work is structured and the different levels of meaning that can occur in a dramatic context. Special attention is given to the tasks that the teachers create in dramatic playing, which are explained with examples from a thematic unit dealing with war and racial discrimination.

Teaching Dramatically examines the crucial role that you, the teacher, play in structuring the drama, negotiating with the class, and working alongside the students in the creation of the dramatic context. Examples of shorter drama activities help identify differing areas in the curriculum where drama can be used to enrich and expand student learning about a topic or issue, and provide illustrations of a variety of drama teaching strategies.

Thinking Dramatically considers ways in which teacher-and-student questioning, writing in role, and observation play an integral role in dramatic playing in terms of learning and the assessment of learning.

REFERENCES CITED

1. Harpe, Sabina. "Children's Conceptions of Drama in Education." M.A. Thesis, University of British Columbia, 1991.
2. Havel, Christopher. "Rifts and Reunions: A Reconstruction of the Development of Drama in Education." In *Living Powers: The Arts in Education*. Edited by Peter Abbs. Taylor & Francis, 1987.

. . . .

INTEGRATING LEARNING

DRAMATICALLY

Negotiating in Play

Too often young children's make-believe play is thought to have little purpose beyond giving the participants a sense of personal satisfaction or gratification, and the opportunity to interact with other children or caregivers. Leading child psychologists and educators have taken a somewhat different view.

"Play," writes L. S. Vygotsky,[1] one of the twentieth century's most prominent writers on language and thinking, "is the leading source of development in pre-school years." According to Vygotsky, children discover the symbolic properties and value of language in their play by themselves and with one another.

In play, therefore, children see one thing but act differently from what they see. Both the situation and the action in the world of play are imaginary, and children create a meaning to guide their actions. A stick becomes a horse, a bundle of clothes is cradled like a baby; so that in play "meaning is separated from the objects that normally embody them, but in real life, this relation is unchanged."[2]

In the following negotiations between Caroline and Sara, both four-year-olds, the children are discussing the glove puppets they have chosen to use in their play with one another:

C: I'm having the princess. Look at her.
S: Ruff, ruff. Hello wolf.
C: It's a wolf. It could be ... a wolf.
S: Well, I'm going to pretend it's a fox.
C: O.K. It can be a fox.

In the process of assigning roles to the puppets, the children also agree on the rules and conventions that will govern their play. In order to keep the princess puppet for herself, Caroline is willing to concede that the wolf puppet is a fox if Sara says so. At the same time, in return for permitting Caroline to keep the princess puppet, Sara establishes her right to make these transformations. ("Well, I'm going to pretend it's a fox.")

In the make-believe play that follows the negotiations, the princess is chased by the fox and then is captured by a wicked witch. (Sara: "Here comes the wicked witch." The fox is transformed into a witch.) After being locked in a castle, the princess escapes with the assistance of her faithful dog (the witch now becomes a dog) and, finally, the witch meets a violent end.

Throughout the play sequence, the transformations of role, context, and content are accomplished jointly by the two children through negotiation. Before the imaginary world is established, they talk *about* their imaginary play and the story they create jointly is developed and sustained through their *negotiations*. (Sara: "I'm going to chase you." Caroline: "Help!" Sara signals to Caroline what is going to happen next and Caroline responds appropriately) and through *narrative*. (Sara: "Here comes the wicked witch!" — introducing a new character.)

In their negotiations both in and out of the pretend frame, the two children work hard to create and sustain the illusion of the make-believe world through collaboration and accommodation, resolving potential conflicts amicably whenever necessary. Working at this spontaneous, intuitive level, the children are already displaying a high level of understanding about the importance of working cooperatively to create their imaginary world.

Working Cooperatively

Working cooperatively is central to dramatic playing, which contains many characteristics of children's make-believe play and places similar demands on students to play together in a spirit of tolerance and acceptance. Although there are fundamental differences between children's self-initiated, make-believe play and the dramatic play of the classroom, it is worth considering what they share in common simply because children who engage in spontaneous make-believe play have already acquired many of the attitudes and skills required to participate successfully in classroom dramatic playing.

In dramatic playing, as in spontaneous make-believe play, there should be:

— A predisposition to engage in dramatic playing and a recognition that for the playing to succeed participants should be self-motivated and self-directed.
— A willingness to cooperate to make the dramatic playing work.
— A recognition that one has to think and act metaphorically in the manipulation of signs and symbols (e.g., a broom becomes a horse).
— A desire to assume and sustain different roles.
— An ability to enter the "as if" world, at the same time recognizing that this is not the "real" world.
— An ability to recognize and understand those non-verbal signs that signal other participants are entering the "as if" world.
— A willingness to help construct and abide by the rules and conventions that govern the creation of the "as if" world.

The common thread running through all these characteristics of play and dramatic playing is social cooperation: the ability of students to work with one another to make the dramatic playing a satisfying and challenging learning experience for everyone in the class. In order to achieve this, you have to provide a clear sense of direction to the class about the sort of *social learning* that you value and wish to encourage.

At a recent meeting of theater arts and drama specialists, which was concerned with drawing up a drama curriculum, I was surprised and delighted to discover that when we pooled those attributes of learning we felt were important to encourage in the drama classroom, the ones dealing with students' developing human relationships were rated as far more important than the learning of technical skills such as acting, stage direction, and stage management.

Here are some of those learning aims relating to social learning:

— To learn to accept the ideas of others.
— To develop interpersonal skills and a sense of group dynamics.
— To know how a group functions.
— To accept different learning styles.

— To identify with other people's lives, their concerns, and
their problems at a personal, concrete level.
— To share their work with others with a feeling of trust and
sincerity.
— To know that what they say, and how they respond, is
valued.
— To assume responsibility for initiating action and ideas.

These aims in drama acknowledge that students should always
be encouraged to view themselves and their contributions to the
work in terms of the needs, interests, and concerns of the other
participants. Fostering positive social attitudes in the classroom
so that learning can take place is a major concern in all teaching. Working with others and learning about others is an important element of any drama. Teachers who use dramatic playing
as a method of integrating learning in the curriculum are providing the foundation for cooperative teaching and learning in their
classrooms.

In order to demonstrate how this is accomplished the next section examines the planning and classroom implementation of a
series of dramatic playing sessions dealing with the theme of
working cooperatively. Although the lessons are primarily concerned with dramatic playing, the content of the dramatic playing is drawn from different areas of the curriculum; so it might
be more appropriately described as an integrated, thematic unit.

Developing a Thematic Unit

In the following sessions, the theme of the dramatic playing is
concerned with the ways in which people work together to serve
the needs of the community: in this case, the creation of a children's neighborhood park. Therefore, the students are not only
learning the value of cooperation *through* their dramatic playing, but they are also learning *about* social cooperation in their
study of the theme itself.

The study of a children's neighborhood park is usually undertaken with seven- to ten-year-olds. However, with adaptations,
the unit can also be used with other age levels.

PLANNING THE DRAMATIC PLAYING

As in any teaching and learning situation, it is difficult to pre-
dict what exactly will occur within the dramatic playing itself

given the spontaneous nature of the work. Therefore, careful consideration of the purposes and aims of the work and the planning of different stages of the dramatic playing will enable you to consider what might happen, and what you wish the students to achieve in their understanding of the issues related to the overall theme.

IDENTIFYING THE QUESTIONS

A useful way to start planning any thematic unit is to identify those questions suggested by the theme and topic, and which are related to the current needs, interests and background experiences of the students.

First, you need to help students identify with the park at a very personal level: the park has to be *their* park. You, therefore, ask questions that lay the foundations for the dramatic playing by seeking information from the students themselves. For this theme, you might like to pose questions similar to the following:

— What purpose(s) should the neighborhood park serve?
— Who should be able to use it? Should there be any restrictions placed on the use of the park?
— What sort of vegetation grows in the park, and what animals and birds inhabit it?
— What are the sorts of problems associated with parks? (e.g., unleashed dogs, vandalism, hurting or scaring wildlife, litter, motorists exceeding speed limits in the park, the homeless)
— Should there be protection for the safety of those who use the park? How can this be enforced?
— Who created the park? Why was it created? How has it changed over the years?
— Who owns the park — the city, the parks board, or the community? How will people know who owns the park? Whose responsibility is it to maintain and preserve the park?
— Should the park always be preserved as a park even though the land may be needed for some other purpose?

These questions can be used in a variety of ways and for different purposes in the dramatic playing including:

— As focus questions to start the dramatic playing.

— As a means of gathering information from the students about their conceptions and knowledge of a neighborhood park.
— To initiate background research into some related aspect of the work (e.g., city bylaws, the function and purpose of a parks board, or park vegetation and wildlife).
— As a basis for writing activities such as journal writing or letter writing.
— As a means of generating more questions that present the students with problems that have to be solved. Who should be allowed to use the park? Should anyone be banned?

Questions are a central component of all dramatic playing negotiations. The questions identified in this preliminary planning require students to think critically and reflectively about the way in which they construct the dramatic context that allows them to explore the overall theme of the integrated unit.

CHOOSING A CONTEXT

The dramatic context establishes the "Who" (the roles taken by the participants), the "What" (what is happening in the drama), and the "Where" (the place where the events of the drama are occurring). This is probably the most critical aspect of the initial planning as you must contextualize the learning in such a way that the interest of your students is engaged. In order to find the most suitable context in which to set the dramatic playing, you might like to ask yourself the following topic questions:

— What fictional roles can students take that will enable them to make use of their own background knowledge, experience, and present level of expertise with respect to the overall theme and topic?
— How will the roles help them identify with the initial focus of the dramatic playing at a personal level?
— Will their roles give them sufficient distance from themselves to enable them to view the work from another point of view?
— How will the events that are occurring in the dramatic playing — the "What" in the dramatic context — give the students a sense of ownership of the drama?

— Will this particular context provide a basis for further exploration of the themes of the dramatic playing?

In the dramatic playing being planned on the theme of "Working Together as a Community" and related to a neighborhood park, a useful way for you to plan a dramatic context is to base it on one or more of the topic questions.

For example, the first three topic questions are specifically concerned with the overall design, purpose, and use of a neighborhood park. Therefore the context in which these questions are examined places your students in the roles of architects and landscape gardeners [the "Who"] being asked to design a neighborhood park [the "What"] by city council at city hall [the "Where"].

So, for the first stage of the unit, you decide that the dramatic context will be as follows:

Who	What	Where
Planners	being asked to submit their designs for a new neighborhood park	at city hall

(This method of determining a dramatic context is adapted from one suggested by Geoff Davies.[3])

Session One: Introducing Dramatic Playing

There are twenty-eight children in this class, and their teacher has chosen to start the dramatic playing by asking them to sit on chairs in a large circle in the center of the classroom. The teacher sits alongside the children in the circle. Behind her is the chalkboard. The children are sitting on chairs because the teacher knows that she wants them to feel that they are professional people coming to grips with a difficult problem.

Because this is their first dramatic playing she works slowly, making sure that they all fully understand that what they are about to do is somewhat different from their regular class work.

First of all she asks them what the word *drama* means to them. Their answers vary: "from being someone else" to "putting on a play." In fact, the words and phrases they suggest to her run the whole gamut of the theater arts including "dressing up," "painting scenery," and "acting." They are all written on the board so that each one of their ideas is recognized as being important.

The definitions provide a springboard for the teacher's description of the type of drama in which they will be engaged. She tells them that all of them will work together to create the drama, and that once they have agreed on what they are going to do and the roles that they will take, they must remain committed to the task. She also tells them she might take a role in the drama too.

"In this sort of drama," she says, "we make up our own stories, and decide together what will happen in the play. Do you think you can manage to do this?" When the children have all agreed, she talks about the drama they are going to do today.

Moving swiftly into the theme and subject of the drama, the teacher invites them to share their stories and experiences of playing in their local park.

"Do most people in your community use the park? Who are the people that you see using the park?" she asks. The children talk about park facilities, the different sort of activities that occur there, and the wide range of people who use the park.

"If," she says finally, "there was one thing you could change about your park what would it be?"

Moving around the circle, the teacher asks each child to say what they might change. Some are ready with a host of suggestions but she limits them to one. Others have no ideas and she says, "So at present you are quite satisfied with your park." In each case she treats their suggestions seriously and with respect, and again she lists all of them on the board.

If there is any child who tries to subvert the work by making a suggestion whose only purpose is to make the other children laugh, she reminds that child of the agreement they have already made to approach the work seriously, and that they cannot continue unless everyone respects that agreement.

Session Two: Selecting a Teaching Strategy

Up to this point the whole class has been working in a mode little different from what they normally experience in the classroom. Now the teacher has to structure the next activity in such a way that they can all move into an imaginary context. Strategies enabling her to do this include:

1. Working through narrative in order to create a story about a neighborhood park in which the students take on roles and explore a problem.

2. Giving the students either a whole class or group activity to do in which they create their own plan for a neighborhood park.
3. Taking a role herself in order to present the students with a problem relating to a neighborhood park.

The teacher chooses to use the third strategy for the following reasons:

— Time has already been spent in carefully preparing the groundwork for the drama. The children want to work in the dramatic playing mode as quickly as possible, and for the teacher to work in role is the swiftest and most efficient way of moving into a dramatic context.

— The teacher has already talked to the class about dramatic playing. By working in role herself she will provide a model for them without having to train them in role-taking skills or telling them how to take a role.

— The teacher recognizes her leadership role in the class. She knows that by taking a role herself and by working within the dramatic context, she will be able to give increasing levels of responsibility to her students once they have demonstrated they can handle it.

— The focus of the drama is on social cooperation. If she wishes to foster this concept within the class, then everyone should participate including her. At the same time, if the students were initially divided into small groups then already the class would be fragmented.

— By working in role the teacher can help the class to maintain a clear focus in their work, always recognizing that at any point in the dramatic playing a need may arise to refocus the work.

Session Three: Taking Roles

Having weighed up all these possibilities before the lesson started, the teacher now tells the class that, if they are willing, she will take a part in the dramatic playing herself. If the students all agree to this, she says that she is going to leave the circle for a few seconds and when she returns she will be someone else. Their task is to work out who she is, what roles they are playing, and respond in role to any questions she might ask them.

These early negotiations in role are similar to those described earlier, when the two girls were playing with the puppets. However, there are two important differences:

— The teacher has already introduced a degree of uncertainty and ambiguity into the dramatic playing similar to that often experienced by theater or movie audiences confronted by an opening scene or shot in which they have to puzzle out what is happening. For the moment, however, the students are protected, like the audience, for they are in a spectator role as the teacher in role speaks to them. When she does ask a question, it will not be directed to any one individual, and they will have the choice of whether or not to answer her.

— In starting the dramatic playing this way, the teacher "owns" the dramatic context (compare this context with the imaginary play initiated by the two girls). She will have to work hard to make sure that the students sense that this is their drama and not hers.

The teacher leaves the circle, and for a few seconds has her back turned to the children. When she faces them again there is a welcoming smile on her face, and she walks briskly back to the circle. She addresses them all briefly: "Good morning, I am delighted you were all able to come to city hall for this important meeting. Let me take a moment to greet you all."

Walking slowly around the circle she shakes hands with every child in the class, establishing the fact that in dramatic playing there is a different sort of teacher-student relationship from that usually encountered in the classroom. At the same time, she has given her students the opportunity to do something in the least threatening way possible, and she has signalled to the class that each of them individually and collectively has a significant and equal role to play in the work.

The teacher limits herself to a "Good morning" or "Good day" so that this opening can be accomplished swiftly. Occasionally, a child responds with a "How are you today?" to which the teacher responds appropriately, but she does not engage in a single, lengthy exchange that might slow down the drama at this early stage.

Returning to her place in the circle, the teacher says in a warm and yet business like tone of voice:

As our time is limited and because I know that you are busy people, I will explain why I have invited you here today as briefly and as quickly as possible. As chairman of the parks board, I have been asked by city council to meet with you and discuss our plans for a special kind of city park. You are probably well aware this city has always prided itself on its parks and the pleasure that they bring to both young and old. All our parks have play areas, sports areas, and picnic areas. Some have other special features that appeal to our older citizens such as extensive flower beds, walkways, and places to sit and enjoy the view.

However, we realize that none of our parks has been designed especially for young people to play in and enjoy. Luckily, we have enough money to create a park especially for the young. That is why I have asked you to come here today. You are the best planners the city has, and we think you could design a park that young people would feel is their own park. There is one condition from the city council: the park should encourage children to know more about the natural environment.

I know that asking you, a group of grown-ups, to plan a park for children is difficult, but I have every confidence that you will be able to succeed. Now before I go on, are there any questions you wish to ask me?

In role, the teacher's initial talk and questions are crucial to the building of the students' belief in the dramatic context. For this reason she carefully scripted what she intended to say in role before the lesson, and learned her words. So as not to forget a key piece of information, the main points were written on an index card, which she checked as she spoke.

There is silence at the end of her lengthy opening speech, and the teacher waits for some time for the first question. She remains silent and does not try to fill the silence with supplementary questions or remarks. Eventually the first question is asked: ''How big is the park going to be?''

Trying not to be too specific, the teacher replies, ''You will be given exact measurements later. Unfortunately, we do not have enough money to buy a piece of land especially for the park, and so we are going to convert one of the parks we already have.''

In answer to further student questions, the teacher assures

them that in planning the park they will be able to include any features they think will help young people appreciate and learn more about the environment. She provides limited information concerning the existing park. For example, it has a lake, few trees, no playgrounds, and largely consists of an open space for walking and playing games. Over the years the park has been neglected.

Still in role as chairman of the parks board, she informs them that the city council expects to see their plan for the new park at the next council meeting, and leaves the circle indicating that the meeting is over.

Returning to the circle as their teacher, she asks the students to think of one thing they would like to see included in the park. After giving them a few moments of silence to reflect, she invites them to say what they have chosen. As the suggestions are called out, she writes them on the board where they will remain until the next lesson.

The list includes:

nature trails	trees
bird houses	tree houses
nesting area	adventure playground
picnic tables	map and guide to wildlife
observation points	flowers
a lake for ducks	sand boxes for little kids
boats	bathrooms
bike paths	ponies
trash cans	petting zoo

REVIEWING SESSIONS ONE THROUGH THREE

Initially, the teacher has taken a fictional role that has the qualities of leadership and authority, one very similar to her own function as teacher. However, she has also an intermediary role, as she does not have the last word in any decisions that are made, and will have to check with the mayor and council who have the power to overrule her and possibly reject the plan.

The roles that the students take as planners permit them to use their knowledge and expertise to tackle the task they have been asked to perform: planning the children's park. Because they are all planners and not taking different roles from one another, she is also signalling to the students that they have equal status in the dramatic playing.

At the same time the teacher talks to the students as "grown-ups" and "planners." If she had asked them to take the roles of children, their fictional roles in the dramatic playing would have been little different from those in their everyday world.

As planners, they will eventually be expected to consider all points of view, not just a perspective which is very close to their own. For example, how will other people, especially adults with no children, react to the decision that one of the existing parks will be turned into a park exclusively for children?

The sort of attitude that the teacher projects now in her role as chairman is designed to make the students in role as planners feel confident that their ideas and their suggestions will be respected and honored. At some future time she may, of course, project a very different attitude, particularly if the city discovers that it cannot fulfil its pledge to create a children's park either through lack of money, or public pressure, or for other reasons.

In telling the students that the kind of park they will be planning will be one in which children explore the natural environment, the teacher has imposed certain constraints on their work that will sharpen the focus of the dramatic playing and, eventually, add more tension. The design of this special kind of park will certainly require careful planning, and will likely involve the students in various kinds of research.

In opening up the meeting for questions from the students before she gives them more information, the teacher hopes that they will ask for some of the details that she needs to tell them before they start planning the park. From the student questions she can also assess their level of interest in the project, discover if they are committed to their roles, and find out if there are any gaps in their understanding of the dramatic playing up to this stage.

By requiring them to answer in their roles as planners, just one or two thoughtful questions asked by one student can help deepen the belief of the whole class. If no one had asked a question, the teacher could have continued to give them more information in role, after telling them to feel free to stop her if they did have any questions.

If no questions are asked, she could stop the dramatic playing and discuss with them their roles as "planners" and the kind of information they need to draw up the park design. However, this is unlikely to happen, particularly in a primary class where children are eager to engage in dramatic playing.

In her answer to the first student's question, "How big is the park going to be?" the teacher is intentionally ambivalent, withholding information about the exact size of the park. (Two of the many skills that teachers have to develop if they wish to work in role is how to ask thoughtful questions and how to respond in such a way that the students feel the need to ask more questions, especially probing ones.)

Finally, the teacher asks the class to make some very concrete suggestions about what they would like to see in the park. In this way the children are able to demonstrate their understanding of the theme of the dramatic playing thus far. In addition, the teacher will be able to use their ideas as a basis for the next stage of the dramatic playing.

Key elements of learning that have been emphasized in stages one through three include:

INTELLECTUAL

Recalling past experiences, thoughts, ideas, relevant information, and images.
Thinking hypothetically.
Making judgments.
Making informed choices and decisions.

EMOTIONAL

Recalling past emotions and feelings.
Expressing personal emotions and feelings.

SOCIAL

Sharing their ideas with others.
Listening to others.
Respecting other people's ideas and opinions.

DRAMATIC

Tolerating ambiguity — when the teacher first speaks to them in role and answers their questions.
Taking a role.
Taking risks.
Understanding the significance of sign and symbol — when the teacher greets them individually in role (sign).

Using reporting language.
Using descriptive language.
Asking questions.
Giving opinions or ratings.
Formulating and establishing hypotheses.
Signalling intentions, and reading and responding to the signals of others.

Session Four: Developing Cooperative Learning

In place of the circle of chairs used previously, the teacher has rolled out a long length of white paper stretching down the middle of the classroom floor. The students' desks or tables are pulled back against the wall, with the children sitting on chairs around three walls. The teacher has listed all their suggestions for the park on a separate piece of chart paper, which is hung at the front of the class.

After explaining that she would like to take a different kind of role to that of the chairman in this next section of the drama, the teacher addresses the class as a colleague. Now that her students have become accustomed to her taking a fictional role, she senses she can signal to them more quickly that she is in role than she did the first time.

Picking up a manilla folder clearly marked *Children's Park* she says:

> Fellow planners, we have a challenging task to perform and one that must be accomplished in a very short time. Therefore, I suggest that we get down to work as quickly as possible. Is everyone agreed to make this project a great success and help one another so that this will be a team effort?

Having secured the students' agreement, she continues:

> I suggest that we first look over the list of ideas that you have already suggested and decide if there is anything you wish to add or alter. Perhaps someone would like to read through the list for us.

While one student reads each item, the teacher accepts suggestions for additions and alterations. When this activity is completed, the teacher asks the class to group the different items in such a way that the park could be planned in different sections. She says:

When I look at your list of ideas it seems to me that some of them would go together very nicely in a part of the park called *Outdoor Recreation* while others might fit into another part that could be named *The Natural Environment*. I wonder if this is a good way of planning the park, and if you have any suggestions of how we could lay out the park?

Several students point out to her that children of all ages will be using the park, so it might be better to divide the park up into different sections for different age levels, roughly corresponding to pre-school, primary, and intermediate. This prompts the teacher to say:

No one has really told us anything about who will be using the park apart from the fact that this is a children's park. Does this mean that any children over the age of twelve should not be able to go? Does this also mean that parents, grandparents or other relatives won't be able to visit the park with their children?

The students discuss these issues at some length. Because they feel that children should not be allowed to play alone and unprotected in a public place, they decide that any child under the age of six who enters the park should be accompanied by an adult caregiver or by an older child preferably over the age of ten.

Finally, it is decided by a show of hands that the park will be planned according to age level. Their ideas for equipment and other items are classified under the following park areas:

Adventure Playground for Primary Children
Nature Theater
Lake Area for Wildlife (accessible to all children)
Forest Area for Birdwatching (accessible to all children)
Picnic Area for Families

Before proceeding, the teacher, still in role, asks the students if they are satisfied with their final list. When they are all agreed, she asks each one to come to the board, and write their names alongside the park feature that they wish to design.

Most children choose to draw the item that they had originally suggested, although some do make different choices. Only one name is permitted to appear alongside each feature.

As a means of checking or validating their list of park features and their designated park areas, the students compile a questionnaire to be sent to other classes in the school in which students of other age levels are asked to say what they would like to see in a children's park that emphasizes the natural environment. Recording the results of this research and compiling bar graphs to show the distribution of choices enables the class to see that their choices are supported by other children.

Now the class is divided into five groups, each group being responsible for one of the five park areas. These groups are composed of children who have already made a commitment to work in one of the five areas.

Before they start drawing the areas, the teacher asks each group to list what they know already about the area they are designing and what they need to know to start their work.

For example, the list for *The Lake Area for Wildlife* reads:

WHAT WE KNOW

There is a lake already in the park.

The lake is surrounded by bulrushes and other reeds.

There are no fish in the lake.

The lake is covered by weed.

There are frogs living in the lake.

There are no trees by the lake.

The lake has to be a place where birds will nest and rear their young.

The lake has to be a place where people can come and see wildlife.

WHAT WE NEED TO KNOW

Should we enlarge the lake?

Should we leave the bulrushes and reeds?

With what fish shall we stock the lake?

Will the fish survive with all the weed on the lake surface?

If we clear the lake of weed will the frogs disappear?

What are the most suitable trees for planting by the lake?

What are the most likely birds to nest by the lake, and eat the frogs, insects, or fish?

How can we provide viewing places for people and not disturb the wildlife?

Walking around each group, the teacher helps the students frame their research questions. When the groups have completed their lists, they read them out to the rest of the class, which makes suggestions of ways in which their questions could be answered. This is followed by further research work in which the group members consult books and other resource materials (see resource list).

To help the groups draw their park area, the teacher takes them to the schoolyard (playground) where they measure the length and width of the area and adjoining sports field. They also measure the play equipment, and identify trees and shrubs growing on the school grounds.

When they return to the classroom, the teacher shows them how to draw a plan of the school grounds to scale in preparation for drawing the plan of the park. After these plans have been drawn and seen by her, she provides them with the over all dimensions of the park area, and the class decides on the scale they will use for the plan.

As soon as each group feels that it has sufficient information to start drawing its area in the park, the teacher gives the group a space on the long roll of paper to work. The group's position has already been determined by the class, which has decided where each area will be situated in the completed park.

Although all the groups work differently, most briefly plan their own area with each student independently drawing his or her item directly onto the roll of paper. When the students have finished their individual drawings, the details of the group's section of the plan are sketched in by all the members of the group. The plan takes some time to complete, and the teacher does not intervene except to answer a question should one arise.

As the lesson draws to a close with the children quietly absorbed in their work, the teacher reads three short poems from a collection of poems called *Prints in the Sand*. The reading of the poems helps enhance the mood of concentration and lends significance to their creation of the park.

I was walking slow
Through the park, trees swayed like
A swan's long neck.

Dave Casperson,
Brookmere Elementary,
Coquitlam.

The touch of sunlight
broke the earth's surface.

April Neufeld,
Nechako North Elementary,
Prince George.

Green, brittle
buds
turn into
meadows
and meadows
of flowers.
Bees rest on the
delicate petals
and snatch the
sticky
nectar.
Birds come back
to hatch their eggs,
and the
leaders
of the
sky
are born again.

Kelly Monahan,
A.S. Matheson Elementary,
Kelowna

Session Five: Developing a Sense of Ownership

Once their drawings are completed the teacher, still in role as
a planner, initiates a series of activities designed to build the
students' feeling of ownership of the park they have created
together. These activities include:
* Walking silently around the plan and looking at other students'
drawings. As they walk slowly, the teacher uses narrative to
heighten the significance of the moment. She says: ''When the
planners had finally completed their work, they surveyed the
finished plan. They saw the brightly colored swings and slides

in the playground, the dark blue of the lake with ducks and geese swimming on the water..." Her narrative and the students' slow procession around the plan gives a sense of ritual to the occasion and helps focus their attention.

* Each group explaining its section of the plan to the rest of the class, and answering first the teacher's questions and then questions posed by other students.

* Envisaging the physical dimensions of the park. Each group of students uses chairs, boxes, blocks, and other materials to create their park area in the classroom working from the plan. When they are finished they have a room-sized three dimensional model of the park area. The teacher asks them to stand outside the park, and look at the model carefully. She asks: "Is there anything that doesn't seem quite right or you wish to change? Think about the distance between different items in your area. Think about the size and height of the different items. Will they be too big for smaller children to use or to look over?" Several students make suggestions about alterations to the plan. One by one they are allowed to enter the park and physically make their recommended adjustment by moving a block or chair. After each adjustment, the teacher asks the student to stand back so that the whole class is given the opportunity to agree or disagree with the alteration to the model. In some cases, other students enter to suggest further adjustments. No final change is made without the approval of the class.

* Preparing to meet with the mayor and council and explain their plan for the park. Here the teacher as planner takes the role of the mayor (role within role) and is shown around the physical classroom size representation of the park. In her role as mayor, she can show students what they might expect when they meet with the mayor and council. The mayor asks difficult questions such as "I don't see any special place for physically challenged children. What are you going to do for them?"

* Identifying those weak areas in the planning that need to be corrected before they meet with the mayor and council.

* Undertaking research that lets the class amend the plans before their presentation to city hall.

* Writing a description of the park and its amenities as part of the final submission. This will be made available to the media.

* Writing personal journal entries about the planning sessions and their feelings about the project.

In a number of ways the teacher has attempted to give her students a sense of individual and collective ownership of the dramatic context. At the same time, she is also preparing them for the moment when the decisions they have made will be challenged by events within the drama (similar to that facing Jennifer in the drama described earlier).

It is this challenge that, at the next stage, will increase the tension of the dramatic playing and present them with a problem that will test their ownership of the plan, forcing them to consider other points of view or perspectives.

Before describing this next development of the dramatic playing, consider some of the steps the teacher has taken in the drama to give all students a sense of ownership of the plan. These include:

— The class as a whole considers all the park amenities suggested by individual students, and gives its joint consent to the final amended list.

— When the teacher classifies individual suggestions under different headings, she seeks class approval and asks for ideas, which are incorporated into the list.

— The class discusses and establishes the rules governing the park's use.

— Each student has to make an individual commitment to complete one aspect of the park by signing his or her name.

— Although the students are divided into groups in order to design their park areas, they work together as a whole class to create the overall plan.

— In their assessment of what they already know and what they need to know in order to design their area of the park, ideas are shared by the whole class about ways in which each group can find the answers to its questions.

— Students have many opportunities to view one another's work and make suggestions and comments.

— The process of drawing a joint plan for the park helps increase students' sense of ownership through the concrete pictorial representation of their ideas. The final product, which is *their* plan, now provides the focus for the drama.

— The activities that follow the drawing of the plan (pages 36-38) are designed to strengthen and support the students' ownership of the plan. When the teacher takes the *role within role* of mayor, the students are expected to explain their ideas and to defend them in the face of "the mayor's" criticism. At the same time, this is only a practice for the formal presentation at city hall. Therefore, the students are protected from feeling that their plan will be rejected out of hand, and are alerted to the fact that there may be difficulties in persuading the mayor and council to accept their plan.

— The group writing and individual writing help the students synthesize their understanding of the dramatic playing up to this point, as well as giving them an opportunity to express their personal feelings and thoughts about the plan.

— Reading through the description of the parks written by the class and students' individual journal entries also provide the teacher with useful feedback about student learning, and their present level of commitment to the dramatic playing.

Key learning elements emphasized in sessions four and five include:

INTELLECTUAL

Being aware of similarities and differences.
Seeing relationships.
Making informed decisions and choices.
Making judgments.
Seeing alternatives.
Thinking hypothetically.

EMOTIONAL

Expressing personal emotions and feelings.
Identifying with the feelings and emotions of others.
Valuing oneself and experiencing a sense of self worth.
Feeling they are empowered to act and make changes.

SOCIAL

Sharing their ideas with others.
Respecting other people's ideas and opinions.
Listening to others.
Incorporating other people's ideas.
Accepting criticism.

Understanding how a group functions.

Going along with and abiding by group decisions.

Knowing how to work with others.

Knowing how to work alone alongside others.

DRAMATIC

Understanding the importance of reflective thinking (writing personal journal entries).

Knowing how to vary pace and tempo.

Appreciating and understanding the use of ritual (the students walk slowly and silently around the plan as the teacher speaks).

Understanding the use of tension (the rehearsal for their meeting with the mayor).

Being aware of the use of space, light, and sound.

LANGUAGE

Comparing and contrasting.

Using descriptive language.

Giving opinions or ratings.

Assessing causes and effects, motives, methods, consequences and implications (discussing the planning and use of the park).

Defending a position (in their group presentations).

NARROWING THE FOCUS

Up to this point the teacher and students have been concerned wholly with the creation and development of the neighborhood park from the perspective of the planners charged with the responsibility of designing it. Even though the students are in role as adults designing a park intended to teach children about the environment, their role-taking has been heavily influenced by the fact they are children planning a children's park. So far they have not had to consider the points of view of other members of the community with regard to the proposal for a children's park.

In order to present the students with a challenging problem to resolve that enables them to move a greater distance from their perspectives as children in their exploration of the central theme of the unit "working together as a community," the teacher considers a number of options available to her.

These differing courses of action are based on the topic questions posed on page 22.

— Who owns the park — the city, the parks board, or the community? How will people know who owns the park? Whose responsibility is it to maintain and preserve the park?
— Should the park always be preserved as a park even though the land may be needed for some other purpose?

Because she has been working hard to help her students feel that the park they have been designing is theirs, the teacher decides to explore the issue of who will own the park once it has been approved by city council. She therefore decides to focus on the following questions:

Who owns the park?
How will people know who owns the park?

In preparing the next stage of the drama, the teacher develops the following dramatic context:

WHO	WHAT	WHERE
An elderly person...	complaining to the planners that she feels excluded...	in the park

Session Six: Exploring Another Perspective

In this lesson, the children are seated on the carpet in a large semicircle. The teacher has asked them to imagine they have walked through the park to the picnic area. The drawing of the park hangs on the wall facing them. The teacher stands by a chair half facing the students and half facing the plan. She speaks to them retrospectively still in her role as chief planner. When she eventually sits down she will assume the role of an elderly person sitting in the park.

The teacher says:

We all remember our excitement at being asked to plan the new children's park. It wasn't an easy task, however, especially when we had to present the plan to the mayor and city council who asked hard and difficult-to-answer questions. Some members of the council thought a better use of the land would be to provide more housing for people who had nowhere to live, but others said, ''Where will the children in

the new houses go to play and learn about the environment
if you take the park away?''

But, after a long discussion, the mayor and council approved
the design for the new park. In six months all the work for
the park was finished, and just before the opening-day ceremo-
nies, the planners came to see their park one last time before
it was filled with children and the park would belong to them.
The park seemed empty as no one was allowed to use it yet.

Changing her tone of voice, the teacher says quietly to the
children:

You have walked through the park as far as the picnic area
where families with children will, in the future, be able to eat
their picnics and play games. If you are standing there what
do you see? What does the picnic area you planned look like
now that it is constructed?

The class is silent for a moment and then several students
describe the picnic area:

There are green picnic chairs and tables.
There's a place for barbecues.
Litter bins.
A pump for water.
A covered place to sit when it rains.
Swings, and a trampoline.

The list continues for a minute or two and the teacher changes
her tone of voice once more, resuming her narrative of their trip
to the new park:

When the planners reached the picnic area, they saw the green
picnic tables, the barbecue pit, the shiny black pump, and
covered building where people could sit when it rained. It all
seemed like the area they had planned for families to enjoy
themselves. However, there was something different; something they hadn't planned for. There was someone sitting on
a bench in the middle of the picnic area. The planners were
very surprised to see someone as they thought the park was
empty.

When I sit down on the chair, I will become that person in
the park. I would like you to watch silently what happens.
When I stand up again, I will not be in role any longer.

The teacher sits down very slowly, smoothes her lap as if she is straightening her dress, looks around very wearily, sighs and places what appears to be a heavy object on the ground beside her.

Then she stands up. The teacher asks the class to describe what sort of person they saw sitting in the picnic area:

A tired person.
Someone with a heavy bag.
Someone who has been shopping and wants a rest.
Someone who is scared.
An old person — and she's unhappy.

The teacher summarizes what the children have told her.

So there, sitting on a bench in the picnic area, is an elderly woman who seems tired because she has been shopping. She puts her bag on the ground beside her. She may be frightened of something or even unhappy. We don't know. So let's see what she does now.

The teacher sits down again, and resumes the same position as before. This time she stretches down as if reaching into the bag on the ground. She takes an object from the bag and places it on her lap. Then with one hand she takes something from her lap and gently scatters it around her.

The teacher stands up again, and asks the class what they now know about the woman. The children tell her that the woman is feeding seed to the birds. This is something that she does each day.

The teacher thinks that perhaps the planners should talk to the woman and find out why she is in the park. The students agree that this is a good idea, and the teacher again sits down. She continues to throw seed to the birds not saying anything. The children remain silent, apparently undecided whether or not they should be asking the first question.

Teacher in role: *Oh, hi there. I didn't see you. You were so quiet that even the birds weren't scared away. Perhaps you would like to help me feed the birds. There's real bird seed in this bag.*

The teacher mimes passing the bag to the student at one end of the semicircle. After this student has mimed scattering some seed, the bag is passed onto the next student and so on around all the class. As this continues, the teacher talks to them intermittently in her role as the elderly woman. Sometimes she makes a comment about herself:

I come here every day, you know, to feed the birds; it's so much better now that there is a lake here,

and sometimes she talks directly to one student:

Throw some more to that mother duck; she has eight eggs to hatch.

When every child has had a turn, the teacher still in role says:

I almost forgot to ask. Why are you here? I didn't think that anyone was supposed to be in the park today.

The children explain to the woman that they are the planners checking out the park, and they ask her why she is there.

The teacher's tone of voice changes.

Teacher in role: *Oh, you're the people who have taken my park away, are you, so that I won't be able to feed the ducks and enjoy the trees and the flowers?*

The children tell her that it isn't her park, that it is for all people who live in the neighborhood.

Teacher in role: *Not from what I hear. I was told that only children and people who have children can come to the park. It's not for old people like me with no children.*

The woman sounds aggrieved, and the children in role try to explain that there are other parks for people like her. The woman says the other parks are too far away for her to walk, and she can't afford a taxi fare as there are no buses. The children try to help her find a solution to her problem, but each time the old woman tells them why what they are suggesting is impossible for her.

When she tells them she has to leave to go home, the students say they will try to help her, and she thanks them.

Out of role, the teacher joins the class. She asks the students to look at the empty bench where the elderly woman was sitting.

Let's imagine the person you talked to is still there. What thoughts are now running through her head now that she has met you, and you have said that you will help her? When you think of something, say it out loud as if you are speaking her thoughts.

The teacher waits, then one child says: "She's probably thinking that we'll go away and forget her."

"Can you say that as if she was really thinking that?" the teacher asks.

They will go away and forget all about me. The child rephrases the sentence **in role**.

Who will feed the ducks when I'm gone? another child says **in role**.

The children continue to focus on the woman sitting in the chair, and speak more of her thoughts.

The teacher summarizes what they have said in narrative.

So the elderly woman left the park and the lake where she used to feed the ducks and geese. As she left she wondered if she would ever return. She also wondered if the planners she had met that day would remember their promise to help her and the other elderly people who liked to walk in the park before it became one for children only.

Now the children are faced with the problem that one section of the community has been excluded from using the park. Out of role, in a class discussion, they reflect on ways that they can help the woman and others like her who will be prohibited from using the new children's park. Finally, in their journals, the students in their roles as planners write about their visit to the park and their meeting with the elderly woman.

Before the lesson finishes, the teacher asks the students to talk to elderly family friends or elderly neighbors they might know about the sorts of things that they do when they visit a park either by themselves or with their friends. Is there something that they like to take with them to the park, like the elderly woman who took a bag of bird seed? Perhaps other older people take a sandwich lunch, a book, or even a camera. Next time, the teacher tells her class, they will see if they can find a way of helping the woman.

REVIEWING SESSION SIX

Throughout the dramatic playing the teacher has emphasized the importance of working and learning together. Therefore, although this session is somewhat different to all of the preceding ones, she maintains the whole–class approach established previously. However, this time the children are seated on the floor, as they are no longer indoors actively engaged in planning the park.

In addition, even though they still remain full participants in the dramatic playing, at several points in this stage of the project, they are also distanced from the work. They listen to the story told by the teacher, and they observe the actions of the teacher in role as the elderly woman.

They remain in role as planners, but they are now going to perform differently. Before, when planning and designing the park, the students were required to draw on their knowledge and understanding of neighborhood parks. Because, in role, they were experts in this field, the parks board chairman needed their expertise. At the same time, the mayor and council had the authority and power to reject their plan.

In her new role as the elderly woman, the teacher has intentionally placed herself in the position of being someone who has little or no power, and who is seeking help from the students to solve her problem.

In contrast to their dealings with the chairman, the students in role as planners can offer only limited help to the woman or they can tell her in no uncertain terms that she cannot visit the park unless she is in the company of a child.

When the teacher tells the children to sit down on the floor rather than stand around the woman and perhaps crowd her, the teacher is placing a physical distance between the children and the woman. This gives all children an equal opportunity to study the woman, and they are not able to dominate her by standing over her.

The narrative the teacher uses to introduce this stage of the dramatic playing provides a link with what has already happened. Because the teacher feels that it is important for the students to examine the neighborhood park from another perspective (in this case, the elderly), she has deliberately omitted including the actual council meeting in which the plan was accepted in the drama, although note that it is mentioned within her introductory narrative.

At this point in the students' first experience of dramatic playing, the teacher wants her class to face an issue that challenges them intellectually and emotionally.

To deepen their dramatic belief in their visit to the park, the teacher asks the students to imagine the picnic area as they planned it, and she incorporates their suggestions into her linking narrative. She deliberately does not tell them who is sitting in the picnic area: this is something that the students will have to work out for themselves.

In her role as elderly woman, the teacher uses only a few carefully selected gestures to signal to the class that she is a woman, and that she is someone of advanced years. She does not *act* the part of a stereotypical old woman. Having an imaginary object to work with (in this case a shopping bag) enables her to focus the students' attention on what she is doing rather than on her.

At the same time, the students are able to participate in role, talking through their verbal, collective description of the woman and their voiced perceptions of what she is doing. In this way they are able to project their ideas and feelings onto the character being created before their eyes. The teacher summarizes what the students have told her, and then includes their thoughts in her portrayal of the woman.

At first, she asks the class to observe her actions in her role as the woman. This gives the students time to concentrate on the woman's actions and formulate their attitudes towards her. By asking them to help her feed the birds, the students are sharing in her symbolic action of caring for wildlife. When eventually the teacher in role speaks to them directly as the old woman, she places the students in a position where they have to explain what *they* are doing in the park. In this way, the students have to do the talking rather than the teacher in role.

The role that the teacher has selected to take is one of a person who feels excluded by society, and is particularly appropriate for this thematic unit on working together as a community. Thus far the dramatic playing has focused exclusively on children and children's needs and interests. Now the students are confronted by someone representing a section of the community whose needs have *not* been considered in the construction of the park. The woman's claim to be included is particularly strong as she exhibits a real love for the park environment, something the park is especially designed to foster in children.

The students therefore find themselves in a situation where there are many parallels in human society of people who feel excluded or discriminated against through no apparent fault of their own. Those parallels that are well within these childrens' past and present range of experience and understanding might include:

— Children who feel excluded because their families cannot afford the money for a class field trip or camp.
— Refugee or immigrant children who arrive at school and

feel excluded and isolated because they cannot speak English.

— Physically challenged students who feel excluded from a class because no provisions have been made in the physical construction of the school for handling their special needs.

— Families with children who are excluded from renting apartments or houses in certain residential areas or complexes (similar to the situation in which these students now find themselves in their dramatic playing).

The teacher has not drawn the students' attention directly to these parallel or analogous situations. However, she might ask them in a future lesson if they can think of any times when they or other people that they know have felt excluded through no fault of their own.

Instead, for the time being, she focuses specifically on the elderly and the ways their needs can be addressed. In this manner, the dramatic playing is moving towards the consideration of a broader, more universal question: "How do people know they belong to a community if they feel their own needs and interests are being ignored?"

Key learning elements emphasized in stage six include:

INTELLECTUAL

Focusing and clarifying images.
Making informed choices and decisions.
Thinking intuitively.
Seeing the implications and consequences of one's choices and actions.

EMOTIONAL

Identifying with the emotions and feelings of others.
Formulating and being aware of personal beliefs and attitudes.
Feeling empowered to act and make changes.

SOCIAL

Sharing ideas with others.
Respecting the ideas of others.
Being aware of and respecting other points of view.
Tolerating differences in others.

Tolerating ambiguity.

Understanding the significance of sign and symbol, for example, by observing the elderly woman and sharing in the feeding of the birds; accepting the empty bench as symbolizing the presence of the elderly woman.

Understanding the significance of projection, for example, by the students projecting their thoughts and feelings onto the actions of the elderly woman; the students project the thoughts of the elderly woman onto the empty bench

Taking and expressing a point of view that might be contrary to their own.

LANGUAGE

Using descriptive language.

Comparing and contrasting.

Asking questions.

Giving opinions or ratings.

Assessing causes and effects, motives, methods, consequences and implications.

Signalling intentions, and reading and responding to the signals of others.

Questioning assumptions.

Defending a point of view.

Stating alternatives.

Planning for Future Sessions

Step by step, the teacher has attempted to create a learning environment and dramatic context in which the students work together as a whole class to face and solve a number of different problems. Working in a manner that respects their knowledge, ideas, opinions, and values, she has introduced issues that are still within their present, personal range of experience.

As these issues become increasingly complex, and move outside the realm of the students' immediate background experience, the dramatic playing is structured in such a way that they will gain fresh insights into the world in which they live.

Before the next session, she has asked them to find out about the needs and interests of the elderly with respect to neighborhood parks. In her planning the teacher has to find a way of enabling students to use their new found knowledge in relation to the over all theme of the integrated unit. So she contextualizes the dramatic playing:

WHO	WHAT	WHERE
Elderly people...	being interviewed by a media reporter...	at the park entrance on opening day.

Apart from the fact that the students have themselves been interviewing elderly people, there are other reasons why the teacher chose this particular context. They include:

— Their new roles will give the students a fresh perspective on the subject of neighborhood parks and the over all theme of working together as a community.
— This activity focuses on attitudes and feelings rather than simply on information. Apart from the previous lesson, in which students dramatized a visit to the park, this is the first session in the dramatic playing that has focused primarily on people's emotions.
— The teacher feels that her class are now ready to play the difficult roles of elderly people truthfully and sincerely because she has already provided a role model for them, and the children have had an opportunity to talk to elderly people who are either friends or neighbors.
— To help them portray their roles as elderly people, each student will be carrying one object that he or she usually takes to the park, and they will be part of a group picture of people standing outside the park (taken for the newspaper) hoping to get in but finding they will not be admitted because they are not accompanying a child.
— In her role as the reporter interviewing the elderly people, the teacher will be able to gauge the students' ability to take different roles and to express different opinions and attitudes from those they may have held previously in their roles as planners. She will also be able to discover the students' level of understanding about the theme of the dramatic playing, and as reporter she will ask them to make suggestions of how the problem could be resolved.

As the unit proceeds, the roles the students take change so that they explore the central theme of the unit from a number of differing points of view and deal with other topic questions that the teacher identified in her preliminary planning (see page 22). In this way, they can examine a broad spectrum of sometimes opposing ideas and opinions related to the question: "How do people know they belong to a community if they feel their own needs and interests are being ignored?"

There are certainly no guarantees that the class will eventually be able to answer this question. However, students will likely have a deeper understanding and awareness of the diverse composition of a community, and the ways in which people cooperate so that everyone experiences a sense of belonging to that community.

This may seem a long way from a class of primary children designing and planning a neighborhood park, but drama, like life, poses tough questions to which there are rarely easy answers. If these questions are either trivialized or ignored in the classroom, then the dramatic playing itself gives children a distorted or simplistic view of reality.

Summary of the Thematic Unit

THEME: Working together to serve the needs of the community.

TOPIC: Designing a children's neighborhood park.

TOPIC QUESTIONS: posed in Sessions One through Six
  What purpose should the neighborhood park serve?
  Who should be able to use the park?
  Should there be any restrictions placed on the use of the park?
  What sort of vegetation grows in the park, and what birds and animals inhabit it?
  Who does the park belong to — the city, the parks board, or the community?
  How will people know who owns the park?
  Whose responsibility is it to maintain and preserve the park?

LEARNING ACTIVITIES (SESSIONS ONE THROUGH SIX)

Brainstorming

  — What students understand about drama.
  — Students' knowledge of parks.
  — One item students would like to see in the park.

Narrating
- Students narrating personal experiences and stories about parks.
- Each group describing its section of the park plan.

Negotiating in Role
- Students as planners talking to the teacher in role as parks board chairman about the proposed plan.
- Students as planners and the teacher in role as chief planner discussing the design and use of the park.
- Students in small groups discussing the ways they will organize their section of the plan.
- Students rehearsing for the meeting with the city council with the teacher in role as mayor.
- Students as planners talking to the elderly woman about her concerns.

Writing
- Students in role as planners writing a description of the park for the media.
- Students out of role writing a personal journal entry reflecting on the planning sessions.
- Students writing a personal journal entry about their meeting with the elderly woman.

Thought Tracking
- Students speaking the thoughts of the elderly woman.

Observation
- Students looking at other students' park plans and reacting to the plans.
- Students seeing the teacher in role as the parks board chairman and working out what role she is taking.
- Students observing the teacher in role as the elderly woman and describing who she is and what she is doing.

Listening
- Students listening to other students' experiences of visits to a park.
- Students listening to other students' suggestions of what features the park might contain.

— Students listening to other students in their small groups as they develop their section of the plan.
— Students listening to other students' suggestions for amendments or alterations to their plans.
— Students listening to the chairman's instructions.
— Students listening to the chief planner's directions.
— Students listening to poetry while they are drawing the plan.
— Students listening to the teacher's narrative about their visit to the park.
— Students listening to the elderly woman's grievances.

Classification

— Students classifying park features according to specific park areas.

Defining Space

— Students working from their drawing to create a classroom-size model of the park.

Estimating Size and Distance

— Students critically surveying and adjusting their model to conform with the plan in terms of the size of different features and the distance between them.

Statistical Compilation of Data

— Students compiling the data from the questionnaire and depicting it in terms of a bar graph.

Drawing to Scale

— Students measuring school grounds to draw a scale drawing in preparation for drawing the park plan.
— Students deciding on the scale of the park plan.

Mime

— Students miming scattering bird seed in the park.

Art

— Students drawing park plan in their groups.

Research

— Students surveying other classes to find out what they would like to see in a children's park.
— Students identifying information they already have and need to know in order to draw the plan; conducting research related to the natural habitat of wild animals and birds as well as other topics that will enable them to plan the park.
— Students identifying weak areas in the plan and conducting research in order to amend the plan.
— Students talking to elderly relations, neighbors, or family friends about their visits to parks.

Group Presentation

— Small groups presenting their sections of the plan to the class.
— Whole class presenting the plan to the teacher in role as mayor during the rehearsal of the presentation to city council.

DRAMA TEACHING STRATEGIES: (SESSIONS ONE THROUGH SIX)

Teacher in role

Parks Board Chairperson: as one in authority seeking expert advice and assistance.

Chief Planner: as facilitator providing leadership.

Mayor: as one in command having the power to make decisions and judgments.

Elderly Woman: as one with little or no power seeking help.

Narration

— Recounting events to heighten the significance of the ongoing dramatic action (e.g., while students in role surveyed the plan of the park).
— Providing a link between present dramatic action and those events that had taken place previously to fill in any gaps in the story, and to move the drama forward, as when the teacher sets the scene for the park visit by talking retrospectively about the presentation to the mayor and council even though it was not actually included in the dramatic playing.
— As a means of incorporating student suggestions and ideas,

as when the teacher narrates the arrival at the picnic area and uses their words to describe the scene.

— To heighten tension and set the tone for the dramatic playing that follows (e.g., in her description of the picnic area, the teacher tells the class that something is not quite right).

— To comment on the story from a different point of view. For example, the elderly woman's thoughts are described in narrative form as a summary of her meeting with the planners in the park.

Mime

— To focus the students' attention on the plight of the elderly woman.

Assessment of Student Learning

Assessment of student learning is ongoing, and related to the five areas of learning: intellectual, emotional, social, drama (aesthetic), and language. The teacher focuses her assessment either on the whole class, the small groups, or the individual student. Assessment is related to the specific learning activities described in the Summary area. Some of these activities, such as writing in role or the drawing of the bar graphs, offer the teacher an opportunity to assess all members of the class individually and provide them with feedback. Other activities, such as the group presentation of the plan, are assessed in terms of the way the group works together, and the individual contribution of each group member.

Other assessment techniques used by the teacher in this unit include:

— Observations of individual students (here the teacher focuses on one learning area and records anecdotal notes).

— Observations of two or three students working together.

— Observations of small groups.

— Observations of the whole class working together.

— Recording spoken reflections of the students.

— Asking students to self-evaluate their work and evaluate the dramatic playing.

— Conducting informal teacher conferences with small groups of students.

More Ideas for Thematic Units

All of the following suggestions could be developed into integrated thematic units following the model described in this chapter. In each unit, students take the roles of people who have expertise facing and tackling problems, or overcoming obstacles. Notice how the constraints that are placed on the roles the students take encourage them to consider the implications and consequences of the tasks they are undertaking.

FOR OLDER STUDENTS USING THE COMMUNITY THEME AND
THE NEIGHBORHOOD PARK TOPIC

— Designing a park that clashes with city council's plans for more housing or parking space.
— Designing a park that reflects the changing multi-ethnic and multicultural nature of the community, and which involves the removal of statues and other commemorative plaques that only celebrate European settlement, development, and domination.
— Cleaning up a neglected and vandalised park in a downtown location, and dealing with opposition from commercial developers.
— Designing an old growth forest park that will preserve the natural environment, but which could deprive loggers of work.

MORE THEMES AND TOPICS FOR PRIMARY LEVEL DRAMATIC PLAYING

— *Helping one another:* a class of six-year-olds all in role as teachers plans an orientation day for next year's class. An anxious prospective student played by the teacher talks to his/her parents, students in role, about the fear of going to school before the orientation, and later visits the teacher, the students in role.
— *Learning about our past:* a class of seven-year-olds in role as dinosaur experts designs and constructs a dinosaur exhibit to persuade a sceptical museum director (teacher in role) that the exhibit should be included in the museum. The director is not convinced that dinosaurs are of sufficient importance to warrant a large, separate space in the museum.
— *Caring for the young:* a class of seven-year-olds in role as poor villagers is hired to look after the baby son and heir

of the king (teacher in role) who has been exploiting them. How do they rear and care for the child so that he will not grow up like his father?

MORE THEMES AND TOPICS FOR STUDENTS AGES NINE TO THIRTEEN

— *Learning about how others lived:* a class of nine-year-olds in the roles of nineteenth century Hudson Bay employees designs and builds a fort in the North West Territories on land deemed sacred by local native Indian people. These events are examined and reconstructed retrospectively by a team of present-day archaeologists, students in role, excavating the site of the old fort. They discover the evidence of Indian habitation by chance.

— *Understanding the nature of change:* a class of eleven-year-olds in role as bronze-age people feel threatened by stories of a startling new technological advance acquired by a rival tribe. A strange looking object (an axe head) is found in the forest. Again this unit could be re-enacted retrospectively.

— *Considering moral choices:* a class of thirteen-year-olds in role as immigration officials investigates the case history of a family (teacher in role as father or mother) claiming refugee status. The parent maintains s/he is in danger of political persecution; extradition papers from the home country suggest otherwise. Here the teacher prepares the extradition papers before the dramatic playing begins.

REFERENCES CITED

1. Vygotsky, L.S. *Mind in Society: The Development of Higher Psychological Processes.* Harvard University Press, 1978.
2. Wertsch, James V., ed. *Culture, Communication and Cognition: Vygotskian Perspectives.* Cambridge University Press, 1986.
3. Davies, Geoff. *Practical Primary Drama.* Heinemann, 1983.

RESOURCE LIST

Here are some recently published children's books that explore different aspects of the natural environment.

Aska, Warabe. *Who Hides in the Park?* Tundra Books, 1986.
Bowden, Marcia. *Nature for the Very Young.* John Wiley and Sons, 1989.

Brownlee, Betty. *The Life Cycle of the Common Sparrow*. Ashton Scholastic, 1992.

Burrie, David. *Plant*. Stoddart, 1989.

Degler, Teri, and Pollution Probe Foundation and Dennis Lee. *The Canadian Junior Green Guide*. McClelland and Stewart, 1990.

Goor, Ron, and Nancy. *Insect Metamorphosis*. Atheneum, 1990.

Heller, Ruth. *How to Hide a Butterfly*. Platt and Munk, 1992.

Lavies, Bianca. *Lily Pad Pond*. Dutton, 1989.

Parker, Nancy Winslow, and Joan Richards Wright. *Bugs*. Morrow, 1988.

Parker, Steve. *Fish*. Knopf, 1990.

Parker, Steve. *Pond and River*. Knopf, 1990.

Suzuki, David, and Barbara Hehner. *Looking at the Environment*. Stoddart, 1989.

Wyler, Rose. *The Wonderful Woods (An Outdoor Science Book)*. Julian Messner, 1990.

PLANNING DRAMATICALLY

First let's take a retrospective look at the thinking that occurred in planning and implementing the integrated thematic unit just described. Then I will emphasize ways in which you can structure students' learning through choice of role, context, and task. To illustrate how you accomplish this, we follow two teachers planning a dramatic playing in an integrated thematic unit dealing with the issues of war and racial discrimination. Their joint class is composed of twelve- and thirteen-year-old students. Particular attention is paid to the tasks each teacher creates for the dramatic playing.

Developing Shared Contexts of Meaning

There are three levels of meaning that teacher and students draw on in their creation of a dramatic context: the *literal*, the *referential*, and the *conceptual*. [1]

The *literal* level of meaning refers to the thinking and language employed by the participants in their construction of the imaginary world.

The *referential* level of meaning looks to those experiences external to the dramatic playing that students use to make sense of this imaginary world in terms of their background personal knowledge, attitudes, and present understandings.

Finally, the *conceptual* level refers to those fresh understandings participants may gain through reflection during or after the dramatic playing experience.

For instance, at the beginning of the unit on the neighborhood park (page 28), the fictional world of the dramatic playing is initially created by the teacher in role as parks board chairman speaking to her class in role as planners. Evoking the feeling that the dramatic playing is occurring in the middle of events, where life is actually in progress, is dependent on the references that the speakers in role make about themselves, other participants in role, and also to those objects and events that have been introduced into this imagined reality. In the case of the meeting between the parks board chairman and the planners, much of the talk concerns the task of creating the new park and their role as planners.

At the same time, out-of-role discussions that take place between teacher and students about the creation of new dramatic contexts is often devoted to the practicalities of deciding on what roles everyone will be taking (who), the time and space in which they are located (where), and the dramatic action (what is happening). Before the children in role as planners meet with the elderly woman in the park (page 42), out of role the teacher asks them to picture the picnic area in their minds and describe it:

> You have walked through the park as far as the picnic area where families with children will, in the future, be able to eat their picnics and play games. If you are standing there what do you see? What does the picnic area you planned look like now that it is constructed?

Some time later, after the children have observed her in role as the elderly woman, the teacher asks the children to describe the woman and summarizes for them what they say in narrative form:

> So there, sitting on a bench in the picnic area, is an elderly woman who seems tired because she has been shopping. She puts her bag on the ground beside her. She may be frightened of something or even unhappy. We don't know. So let's see what she does now.

The language that is used by the teacher and by students on both occasions at this literal level of meaning is specific, practical, and concerned with either what is going to happen or what is actually happening within the dramatic playing. Whether the teacher and her students are working in or out of role, this careful construction of shared contexts of meaning at the beginning of each stage of the dramatic playing provides a solid foundation for the work that will follow.

When the class in role as planners talks to the elderly woman they can use the language of their profession, and they can either repeat or refer to some of the arguments that have already been considered in their rehearsal of the demonstration of the park plan to the teacher in her role within role of mayor. You will recall they try to reassure the woman that there are other parks for people like her (page 44).

However, by continually pressing the students to find ways to help her rather than just repeating the "official" arguments of city hall, the teacher in role as elderly woman is now throwing the students back on their own personal resources. The manner in which they speak to her and treat her, the kinds of response they make to her plight, the attitudes they project, and their ability to gauge what she might be thinking and feeling are based not so much on the knowledge they may have gained as park planners but on their personal qualities and their social and cultural experiences. At this referential level of meaning, the focus of the dramatic playing is on social relations, emotions, and feelings. Equally importantly, the focus is also on higher level thinking in the intellectual area of learning.

Here again are some of the key elements of the intellectual, emotional, and social areas of learning described at the end of the review of session six (page 48).

INTELLECTUAL

Focusing and clarifying images.
Making informed choices and decisions.
Seeing the implications and consequences of one's choices and
    actions.

EMOTIONAL

Identifying with the emotions and feelings of others.
Formulating and being aware of personal beliefs, values, and
    attitudes.
Feeling they are empowered to act and make changes.

SOCIAL

Respecting the ideas of others.
Being aware of and respecting other points of view.
Tolerating differences in others.

The *referential* level of meaning in dramatic playing, therefore, draws heavily on the participants' understandings about themselves and the world in which they live. At this level, students are being encouraged to make connections between their external experiences in the "real" world and the issues they face in the imaginary world of the drama.

Any connections they do make, leading to new levels of personal understanding and different ways of approaching a problem or issue, occur at the *conceptual* level of meaning. Referring back to the integrated thematic unit in the previous chapter, at the end of session six (page 44), the teacher asks the students to speak out loud the thoughts of the woman. This reflective activity is intended to help the students adopt and express another point of view. It also may help them to come to grips with some of the broader moral and social questions posed in the unit. Equally importantly, the activity helps the teacher to assess whether there has been a change in her students' thinking and understanding of these issues.

Planning the Task

As I indicated earlier, by taking new roles and working in differing contexts as the dramatic playing progresses, the teacher of the neighborhood park unit attempted to give her students a range of perspectives that can expand and strengthen their conceptual level of understanding. In her planning of the dramatic playing, she also gave careful consideration to the task or tasks that the students will undertake in role.

Initially, the task the students faced as planners was to design a neighborhood park for children and their families that would teach the children about the natural environment. The terms or conditions of the task itself placed constraints on the children working in their roles as planners, eventually requiring them to consider the implications of designing a park that excluded certain people visiting it.

The seeds of the tension that developed in the dramatic playing (that is, the conflicting interests of the council which had commissioned the planning of the park and those of the elderly woman) were already sown in the task that the planners were asked to perform. Notice, however, that the planners did not themselves create the conditions that governed the task; these were imposed on them as a condition of being given the planning contract.

When they meet the elderly woman in the park, the children in role as planners are not placed in a situation that can only result in open and direct confrontation with the elderly woman. Instead, they find themselves negotiating with the woman within the limits of certain constraints. Although the woman appears to think they have the power and authority to help her, the planners know their power is limited even though they may sympathize with her plight. The most they can do is to offer to help her. If they did have the power to make the decision to permit her to use the park, then the solution to the problem could have been very easy — too easy, in fact — and the story might have had a neat, but rather simplistic, happy ending. As it is, when the woman and the planners do part, her problem is still unresolved, providing teacher and students with opportunities to explore the dilemma further from a number of different points of view or perspectives and, of course, to pursue a different kind of task: addressing the needs of the elderly woman.

WITHHOLDING INFORMATION TO INCREASE TENSION

Earlier I suggested a number of different topics for dramatic playing that could be developed into integrated thematic units. Most of these suggestions involve tasks to be performed that contain certain conditions and constraints, and confront students with problems that involve making choices. Constraints and choices also face you, for you need to decide how much information to give students and how much to withhold, thus increasing the tension of the dramatic playing and helping students reach new levels of conceptual understanding.

However, your planning of any dramatic playing needs to be sufficiently flexible to allow opportunities for the unexpected to occur and fresh directions to be explored. Only today, for example, a teacher described to me some dramatic playing that had absorbed her class for the whole school day. In role as designers or architects the six-year-olds had planned a new extension to their school (some of our local schools are desperately overcrowded). Rather than informing them from the outset that their designs or plans had to be environmentally "friendly," the teacher in role as a school board member left this question until after the children had started drawing their plans in pairs. Instead, she told the class that a group of experts in designing schools would select the one they decided would be most suitable.

Moving around the class in her role as a school board member, the teacher casually asked each pair, among other things, if they had considered how their building would affect the environment. She was surprised and delighted to discover that all the children had taken this into account; so much so that when each pair of designers presented their plans to the experts (the rest of the class in role), their final selection was based largely on environmental criteria.

She knew her class wanted to continue with this topic in their dramatic playing but was unsure of what to do next to challenge them. It so happened that the winning design was built on stilts at third floor level, and I suggested that she might take the role of some important visitor eager to see the new extension but with no head for heights (the extension had to be entered by stairs from the outside). In this way the class would have to address two other factors in their design: safety and, equally important, the use of the building by someone with a disability. Both are important environmental issues of another kind that might conflict in some ways with their primary concern to protect the natural environment. Because the visitor's disability is not immediately visible, the students would have to discover this for themselves. In this way the teacher in role can withhold information that will increase the tension of the dramatic playing and confront the children with a challenging problem to be solved.

Background to the Planning

To give you some sense of how you can plan a dramatic playing in which information is deliberately withheld and students in role are asked to perform a task, I give the example of two teachers discussing some dramatic playing they are about to implement with their combined classes of twelve- and thirteen-year-olds. The forty children, whom they team-teach, include children from diverse ethnic backgrounds, some of whom are immigrants from other countries. For many of these students English is not their first language, but they are all now fluent in the language.

Although there does not appear to be any racial friction among students in the class, the teachers feel that examining race relations should be an integral part of their curriculum. At the same time, because of the varied background experiences of their students, they also wish to explore with them what it is like to be a child whose life is uprooted by war, discrimination, and persecution. In this class the reading of children's books and the study of literature are important components of the language arts program, which is combined with social studies. Dramatic playing is the tool the teachers will use on this occasion to integrate the various elements of reading, writing, listening, and talking with the content of social studies.

The teachers, Diane and Stephen, have decided their class will examine the issue of racism from a historical perspective to allow for some level of distance and detachment on the part of the students. They believe that dealing with a current issue might be too emotionally charged, and would not allow for the kinds of critical thinking and reflection that they wish to encourage in their students at the conceptual level of understanding.

The topic they have chosen to examine concerns the deportation of Canadians of Japanese descent from the Pacific coast of Canada to internment camps in the interior during the Second World War. (Similar deportations of Americans of Japanese descent, of course, occurred in the United States after the bombing of Pearl Harbor in December, 1941, and with some modifications the dramatic playing that follows could be used as a model for the exploration of this parallel historical situation.) In fact, if one considers the many instances of racial discrimination and persecution that have occurred during times of war and the literature that deals with these issues, there are many opportunities for exploring this topic through dramatic playing, *The Diary of Anne Frank*[2] being but one of the most famous examples. Other suggestions for related source material are listed on page 125.

Before the teachers start planning the dramatic playing, here is a short historical background to the deportation of Japanese Canadians. My source is *The Canadian Encyclopedia*.[3]

> In February, 1942, the Canadian government ordered the deportation of 20 000 Canadians of Japanese descent and lineage from an area of 160 km within the Pacific coast of British Columbia. The deportation was carried out in spite of opposition from senior officers of the Canadian military and Royal Canadian Mounted Police who maintained that Japanese Canadians posed no security threat. After leaving their homes, which were sold by the government along with their farms,

businesses, and personal property, the internees were held in livestock barns on Vancouver's Pacific National Exhibition grounds. Later they were transported by rail to camps in the interior. Towards the end of the war, Japanese Canadians were forced to choose between deportation to Japan, or moving east in Canada. Even after the war, laws were still in place preventing them from taking up residence again on the West coast. A number of British Columbians living on the coast profited from the dispersement and acquisition of Japanese Canadian land and property.

THE PRELIMINARY PLANNING SESSION

For the past month Diane's and Stephen's class has been reading about and researching the deportation of Japanese Canadians in the Second World War. In addition to reading copies of contemporary news reports and non fiction books written on the topic, they have been collecting and studying photographs, diaries, and other related material. They have also interviewed local Japanese Canadians whose lives were in some way affected by the deportation. In addition to reading Sheila Garrigue's *The Eternal Spring of Mr. Ito*,[4] many of the students have read Joy Kogawa's children's novel *Naomi's Road*,[5] based on her adult novel *Obasan*,[6] and Yoshiko Uchida's *Journey Home*,[7] which tells the story of the internment of Japanese Americans. However, much of the language arts instruction has been focused on one book: Shizuye Takashima's *A Child in Prison Camp*.[8] Takashima is an artist who, as a child, was deported with her family from Vancouver to New Denver. Her memories of those painful years are poignantly depicted in haunting word pictures and the delicate pastel shades of her childlike paintings. Diane is particularly fond of this book which she read as a child, and wants to transmit to her students some sense of the way it altered her view of the world. However, she realizes that Takashima's story is told in deceptively simple language — the imagined language of the child — and has therefore suggested to Stephen that they explore the text further through dramatic playing. This will be the first time that Stephen has used dramatic playing in the classroom.

Stephen: Why drama? What with forty kids, and all the bookshelves, tables, and chairs, there's not much room to move anyway, and I can just imagine the mayhem once they start charging all over the place.

Diane: The reason I want to use drama, or dramatic playing really, is I'd like to see how they interpret the book in another medium, particularly an artistic medium. After all Takashima is an artist. I really don't think simply writing about the book or even discussing it has helped them to see some of the subtleties of the text.

Stephen: I know what you mean about the subtleties of the language. There are so many layers of meaning in the story which I think the kids may have probably missed when we were reading the book to them in class. I thought that moment when she describes standing by the railway tracks before dawn waiting to leave Vancouver was particularly striking and very moving. She's looking with a young child's eyes at the beauty of the landscape, thinking about her friends she's leaving behind, and at the same time sending us all kinds of messages about being whisked away from the Pacific National Exhibition to the tracks before the city awakes, and then having to wait around for hours without food before the train arrives. There's so much dignity amidst all the indignity that is being heaped upon them.

Diane: That's exactly the point I'm making; not only can you see what she's telling us either consciously or perhaps even unconsciously, but you've also got the language to express your ideas. I think dramatizing the book will help the class to look more closely at the text, and give them a real purpose for teasing out some of those hidden messages. It's almost like hearing the voices that are there in the book.

Stephen: Voices?

Diane: Well, I call them voices for want of a better description. You remember that passage just before they leave Vancouver? Her dad writes to her mother from the camp in the interior that he is being moved to a smaller camp eighteen hundred feet above sea level. Here's what Takashima writes: 'The Government wants the Japanese to build their own sanatorium for the T.B. patients. I hear there are many Japanese who have this disease, and the high altitude and dry air are supposed to be good for them.'[8] Who is really speaking there? What voices are we hearing? Takashima as an adult writing to recreate her childhood voice? Her dad writing to her mother echoing the official line of the government because he doesn't want his letter censored, or what? It happens all the way through the book and shifts from sentence to sentence so we hear all those different voices.

Stephen: But isn't it *you* who hears them in a very personal way? I'm not sure how drama or dramatic playing is going to help the students hear them and become more aware of all those hidden messages.

Diane: Well, I've always been struck by the visual quality of the writing, and I believe the book lends itself to dramatization especially because it is so episodic. I would hope that being faced with the challenge of having to create scenes from the book will compel the students to look more closely at the text. I am hoping that their depictions of various incidents from the story will not only deepen their own understanding, but also allow us to see how they are responding to the different layers of meaning. After all, we've been immersed in all this other material for the past month and heard Japanese Canadians recount their experiences, too, plus the fact that a few of the kids have had similar kinds of experiences in refugee camps.

Stephen: O.K., I see your point, but why don't we give them a *purpose* for dramatizing the book? A video or film would be a really good way of focusing their attention on the visual aspect. At the same time, there are all kinds of techniques they could use such as voice over, speaking someone's thoughts, and so on.

Diane: That's a great idea. Let's say they are in role as T.V. directors, producers, and scriptwriters, then they would have to look at the book from a visual perspective. They would have to make decisions about which scenes they were going to include and which to leave out, and they would have to decide in what order the scenes would be placed to have the greatest impact.

Stephen: Yes, and the story could be seen and told through the eyes and voice of a child.

Diane: But of course we want to hear those other voices, too, those that might conflict with what she is saying.

Stephen: Yes, that would be very effective, but don't let's try and write the script for them; let's see what they come up with. On the practical side, do we have enough copies for them all?

Diane: Not really. There are half a dozen copies I borrowed from the school and local libraries, plus my own copy. I was originally thinking they would work in small groups of four so we would have ten scenes from the story with a linking narrative. Each group would create one scene based on an extract they copied from the book.

Stephen: Well, we can still do that with the video or film. As a class we could all storyboard or plot the film together by selecting scenes from the book. Then we could ask the groups to help one of us type the extracts they have selected from the book as a basis for their particular scene onto the class computers. After all, they will probably only need one or two paragraphs. The books could be used for reference if a group needs more detail.

Diane: So where do you think we should start?

Stephen: Perhaps first we should find out just how much they know about making a movie. I can handle that if you start the dramatic playing.

Diane: O.K. You do the brainstorming, and I'll work in role with them. As they are going to have to create a script, I think you should focus on writing for the screen. That means we can move into the dramatic playing quite quickly. So, if you prepare the first session, I'll take care of the second one.

Session One: Brainstorming the Topic

From Diane's Journal

I have to admit I was rather nervous about this first pre-dramatic playing session. I've worked with a number of these students before in role, but Stephen admits he doesn't know anything about dramatic playing. He promised that he wouldn't actually tell them what we are going to do, and I hoped he wouldn't let it slip inadvertently. So much depends on the element of surprise in this work.

However, I had no need for concern. There was something almost theatrical about the way Stephen caught their attention right from the start. When the kids came into the class, they found their tables pushed back and a long roll of white paper running down the length of the room on the carpet. Instead of going to their tables, Stephen asked them to stand quietly on either side of the paper so that there were two long lines of kids facing each other, and he stood very calmly at one end of the paper, not saying anything more, just waiting for them to concentrate on being quiet. If there's one thing I have learned in dramatic playing it's being patient, and just waiting for things to happen.

Then Stephen started telling them we were going to do something different today, although it was still connected with our work on Japanese Canadians. Immediately, I could see one or two looking at me. I'm sure the roll of white paper had triggered their memories about the dramatic playing unit on the neighborhood park we had done together two or three years back. I carefully avoided giving them any hint that I knew what was going to happen next; this was Stephen's session and he didn't need any distractions. I was just praying the P.A. system wouldn't interrupt the atmosphere of anticipation that I could already sense in the room.

Then Stephen spoke to them. He explained that for the next part of our work it was very important for him to know how much the class knew about making movies, especially writing for the movies. He then asked each student to work with the person facing them. Together, each pair would compile a list of all the words they knew associated with making movies, especially screen writing. Again a nice choice of words and task; we were already into the vocabulary and students could work together. He also asked the pairs to talk quietly to each other so that the pairs working next to them could concentrate on their lists.

Kneeling or sitting down on the carpet the students started creating their lists of words together. Stephen set it up so that only the students on the right side of the paper did the writing. I realized that meant we would have twenty lists which could be later taped to the wall.

I was pleased to see the concentration of each pair and amused to see how one or two partners traded places so that the better writer or speller actually did the writing, but that was O.K. They must have worked for at least fifteen minutes on their lists, and I could see that a number of them knew quite a lot about movies or T.V. films. Even those who didn't have the vocabulary to describe what they knew invented their own terms. So "panning shots" became "moving shots" and "long shots" became "distant shots," but it was good to see them struggling to find the language.

When a few of the pairs had finished their lists, Stephen told them they could walk around the paper and look at other people's lists. This was a bit tricky because of the lack of space, but they were so interested in what everyone else had written that there were few problems. When every pair had finished, the sheet was taped up to one end of the classroom, and everyone had a chance to see what had been written.

Stephen guided them skilfully through the long lists, asking each pair to imagine they were teaching us about writing for the movies by selecting one term they had written down that no one else had included, and describing what it meant. While this was going on I compiled a list of the terms they had selected. If there was debate over the exact terminology, the different words were starred, so they could be checked later. Stephen didn't try to correct them. The final list we came up with just about covered everything it seemed to me, and Stephen admitted he was surprised how much they knew. Here is the final list the class compiled together and classifed under different headings, with a little bit of help from some useful resource books. Against each term we placed a brief definition.

WRITING FOR THE MOVIES[9]

The Parts of a Film

frame — a single shot on a length of film.
shot — a single continuous portion of film.
scene — a series of shots showing actions in one location.
sequence — a series of scenes leading to a climax.

Transitions

cut — an instantaneous transfer from one shot to another.
dissolve — the gradual merging of the end of one shot into the beginning of the next.
fade-in — the gradual emergence of a shot out of darkness.
fade-out — a shot gradually disappears into darkness.
cut-away — a shot of something other than the main action.
cut-in — a shot inserted into the main action.
editing (cutting) — the process of assembling the shots into their final order, and of cutting them to their final length.
take — the single recording of a shot.

Camera Perspective

camera angle — the angle from which camera views subject.
  high angle — camera looks down on subject.
  low angle — camera looks up at subject.
  flat angle — camera at same level as subject.
camera distance — the distance between camera and subject.
long shot (LS) — shows the subject at a distance. Also known as "the establishing shot," because it shows the subject in relation to its general surroundings.
close shot (CS)/close up (CU) — shot taken close to a subject to reveal detail
medium shot (MS) — shot that falls between a long shot and a close shot. This shot shows the main subject in relation to its immediate surroundings.

Camera Movement

panning — tripod remains in place but camera rotates from left to right or right to left.
tilt — tripod remains in place but camera moves up and down.
zoom — camera remains in place but seems to move quickly toward or away from the subject because of action of zoom lens.
dolly (truck) — the camera itself moves on tripod toward or away from the subject.
travel — the camera moves on a tripod parallel to moving object. (Follow shot)
boom — the camera dips subject from any angle (the camera is usually mounted on the end of a hydraulic arm).

The Sounds of a Film

human speech
  dialogue — the speech between characters in a film.
  monologue — either spoken or thought aloud.
  commentary — the descriptive talk accompanying a film.
sound effects — the noises connected with the action being depicted.
music
  realistic — music that is part of the action being depicted (e.g., a band in a parade).
  functional (background) — music added to produce an emotional effect or to provide continuity.

Shooting Script
plot — a brief outline stressing high points and climax.
characters — dress
camera set-up — for each scene involving: distance; height;
  angle; movement of camera; duration of scene.

At the end of the day, Stephen asked the class to watch T.V.
for about half an hour that evening, and note down the ways
in which the camera was used. He suggested that they not all
watch sitcoms or music videos but look at documentaries, too,
as this would be very useful for the next part of our work. There
were two kids who had no T.V. sets and no access to one. He
suggested that they look at books with photographs in them,
again noting down how the camera might have been used.

Planning for the Dramatic Playing

From Diane's journal
Stephen agreed to lead a discussion about the students' viewing experiences at the beginning of the next session, which would
then lead into my dramatic playing session with them. I have
to admit that I was quite anxious about the whole thing. The
kids seemed to know so much about T.V. production that I didn't
see how I could really teach them anything they didn't know
already. I calmed down, thought about the book again, and realized that really the main purpose of the whole exercise was to
look with different eyes at the story.
  Somehow I had to create a task and context that would give
them the opportunity to find that fresh perspective or "lens."
Rather than asking them to take roles, which could have resulted
in losing or obscuring this focus, I started thinking about some
of the most powerful images that the book conjured up in my
mind. There were so many that again I started feeling swamped.
Then I remembered the question we had posed at the start of
the unit: "What is it like to be a child in times of war when you
are persecuted and discriminated against?"
  At that moment, I realized that the initial focus had to be on
the child, and the film they were about to create also had to focus
on the eyes and voice of the child. Takashima's age at the time
of the deportation appeared to be about the same age as our
students, although she admits she pictures herself two years

younger than she really was. I had to find a moment with which all the students could personally identify with a child of their age. Of course, it could be the longing to be in high school but I felt that was a bit trivial, and then I thought of her leaving the New Denver internment camp with those mixed feelings of excitement about the future, and sorrow at having to leave behind her beloved mountains.

I also thought about her picking up her sister's gift of the "Dutch shoe" the night before the family departed, and all the memories the gift evoked in her. Here was the moment I needed to help crystallize the pain and joy of leaving for a child. I also hoped that this might help the class to recall those moments in the book that really stood out for them, which might form the basis of the plot line for the film. In fact, this moment could actually be the start and end of the film itself. Again my imagination and tendency to predetermine what should happen next were running away with me. No, this had to come from the students as much as possible. So my plan started taking shape.

OPENING ACTIVITIES

Students sitting at their tables are asked to think of one possession (object, not animal) they own that has special meaning for them. The possession does not have to be valuable, just something they value very highly because of the memories that they associate with it.

Now they have to move their chairs so that they are not facing anyone, and so that they have space to work and can stand up and reach out if necessary.

I want them to imagine they are picking up this object and putting it away for the last time. They are leaving their home and cannot take it with them. The whole action should be done slowly so they have time to think about the feelings and memories they associate with their belonging.

Once they have finished, they can turn and talk to a partner about the object, their memories, and any feelings they have about leaving it behind.

As a wrap-up to these opening activities, students are invited, if they wish, to talk about their possessions to the rest of the class. Just in case some don't want to disclose what they chose, it seems better to give them a choice.

Session Two: Finding a Focus

From Stephen's journal
After the class and I had discussed their observations of T.V. camera work the night before, Diane started her dramatic playing. I wasn't at all prepared for what happened. The kids were completing absorbed in miming: picking up, inspecting, and putting away their possessions. Some even took the object out for a second look. You could hear a pin drop. It was a really good idea not to have them facing anyone.

When they talked about their memories and possessions to the rest of the class there was no holding them. There was Rashid, for instance, from a town in the Middle East, who had been cooped up in an apartment for a year with his mother with the drapes closed most of the time. Neither of them dared to look out and show themselves at the windows. He remembers the glass on the picture on the wall which sometimes caught the reflection of the outside world when the drapes were open just for a few brief moments at a time. When they were going to leave he took the picture down to stow it away in his bag but his mother told him to put it back. That's what he did in his mime: taking down and putting back the picture. He couldn't even remember exactly what was in the picture — mountains and a lake he thought. Of course, not all the stories they told were that dramatic but everyone had to have his or her say.

After that very intense opening, I wondered if Diane's next activity would really hold their attention. I was hoping it would as it had to lead directly into the screen writing. She told them that the whole class would work together as if they were screen writers creating a scene.

She briefly reminded them of the end of Takashima's story and then read this paragraph:

Mother and I begin to pack. I have to leave many things I have grown to love behind. My favorite "Dutch shoe" which Yuki gave me almost two Christmases ago is still by my bed, on the narrow shelf near the candle. I pick it up. The candies and nuts are gone. The sparkly, gold rice is dull, many grains have already fallen off; more drop into my hand. But as I hold it I can still feel the love the kind Sisters put into it just when we needed love so much. I placed it back on the shelf. It is too fragile to pack.[8]

Diane's tone of voice changed.

"If," she said, "we had to recreate that scene here and now, what could we use to represent Shichan's 'Dutch shoe'?"

There was silence,

I had been expecting Diane to produce something resembling the "Dutch shoe" out of her bag like a magician taking a rabbit out of a hat.

Just when I thought no one was going to do anything, a girl ran up with a shiny black boot. Diane gestured her to set it on an empty, narrow table she had placed in the middle of the room.

The girl sat down, and Diane asked the class if they were willing to accept this as the shoe. If not, they could try something else. Slowly the students seemed to be warming to the task. A rapid succession of different objects were placed on the table and then removed by someone else. No one seemed satisfied.

Diane just waited.

Then almost as if by magic a faded yellow block of wood appeared on the table. Suddenly the exchange of objects stopped. Diane waited and then asked them: "Are you prepared to accept this as 'the Dutch shoe'?" The kids nodded.

Diane started talking again.

"The time has come for Shichan and her mother and father to leave the camp. This is their last morning. The family's cases are packed. Before you is the house where they have lived for the past two and a half years. Would someone show us where the door is through which they will leave?"

A boy came up and stood by the table with the "Dutch shoe" on it. Diane asked the class if they thought that was where the door should be. There was some discussion and finally "the door" was shifted to one side. The boy sat down, and some students asked if two chairs could be placed to represent the door. The others agreed; so Diane placed the chairs in position.

"Do you think we need anything else to help us believe this is the house?" she asked them.

After further experimentation, they chose a small mat placed in the middle of the room, and a candle which was placed in a cup some distance from the "Dutch shoe" on the table. Three cardboard file boxes, representing their packed possessions, were piled by the door.

By this time the classroom was very quiet.

Diane asked the students to decide who would be in the room

and where they would be. She also asked them to describe their physical positions.

They decided that Shichan would be by the table, hand stretched out, touching the "Dutch shoe" gently. Anyone was invited to take that role and one of the girls volunteered. Slowly the scene was created with the father looking through the door at Shichan who was turned away from him. The mother knelt down by the boxes strapping up the last box.

The scene was very powerful, and now I could see why Diane had not created a "Dutch shoe." The intensity of feeling we all seemed to feel at that moment was far more "real" than a scene that faithfully reproduced all the details described in the book.

Diane now used a number of interesting techniques to "bring the scene to life." The students who were observing were asked to say what each of the characters might be remembering as they stood there poised to go. They were also asked to give each of the three people a line to say so that the frozen scene came to life. They tried this several times with all sorts of variations. What really caught my attention was the way the class handled the spoken thoughts and memories of the three people. I could hear the mixture of bitterness and relief in the voices of the father. There was relief also in the mother's voices, but there was also a sense of joy and anticipation as she looked forward to seeing her other children again. [At this stage in the story, her other children are in Ontario.] As for Shichan her tone was quieter and quite restrained as if she had grown a lot during her internment. Perhaps this was what Diane had meant about hearing the voices in the book during our first discussion.

Finally, Diane asked the class to break into groups of four, and write their own shooting script of those few moments including, if possible, the directions they would give to the camera crew about the different kinds of shot and camera angle. We had decided that their first attempt at a script should be kept simple, without many restrictions being placed on their writing it like a professional script. The groups worked well at this for the rest of the morning, and both Diane and I were eager to see their first attempts at script writing.

REFLECTIONS ON SESSION TWO

From Diane's Journal
When we started today I really hadn't expected to work at the

dramatic playing for most of the morning but I think we were right not to break and come back to it later. We seemed to have traveled a long way. I was particularly pleased with the building process of working with very concrete, specific things of the film vocabulary first, then moving into their experiences of watching T.V., their possessions and memories, and finally putting it all together in the scene at the house in New Denver.

I really think that, if we were to stop now, much of what we had hoped to accomplish in terms of helping the students to look at the book with a fresh perspective has happened.

I think I have learned a lot, too. Setting the class very clear tasks that everyone could understand was very important to the success of the work, and I was particularly pleased with the way they all worked together. There were no control problems. In fact it almost seemed as if the class controlled itself in response to the tasks they were given. Obviously this is a class that can work by itself in spite of its size if it is sufficiently motivated.

This means we shall have to find fresh challenges in the dramatic playing after they have finished their scripts of the scene. I'm already thinking of ways in which we could create a situation where they present their shooting scripts to the representative of a large broadcasting corporation (perhaps with Stephen in role for the first time) who is interested in commissioning a movie of what it is like to be a child in time of war, but is worried about offending various members of the viewing public, particularly those who still remain unconvinced that the Japanese Canadians suffered any injustice. In that way, the students in role will be faced with the choice of either trying to convince the executive that their script and the material with which it deals should be brought to the attention of the public, or offering to alter their script to make it more acceptable to viewers. They might, of course, reject the offer outright, and then Stephen in role will have to consult with his board to prepare a counter offer. It would be very interesting to see if the students themselves could take the roles of the board members to give them yet another perspective. But here I am again trying to predetermine what will happen.

I really think this class is ready to undertake these kind of tasks particularly after hearing some of the personal experiences today and seeing the sensitivity and concentration with which they worked. It seems a long way from my discussion with Stephen

when we both wondered if there would be sufficient books to go round!
End of Journal Entry

In the opening sessions of the dramatic playing just described, you will have noticed that the teachers moved to dramatic playing more indirectly and obliquely than in the integrated, thematic unit described earlier, when teacher and students almost immediately assumed roles within the dramatic context. Because the dramatic playing of the plight of children in wartime focuses on emotions and feelings, structuring activities allow the students to reflect first on their own personal experiences and feelings before Diane leads them to bringing "the scene to life." In this way, Diane, with her knowledge of dramatic playing, leads her students to make connections between their own feelings and those of Shizuye Takashima and her parents.

The kind of challenge that Stephen now faces of teaching in role for the first time is addressed next, when I will explore the ways you can structure your students' learning from inside the dramatic playing.

REFERENCES CITED

1. The different levels of meaning are based on those described in Bernard Beckerman's *Dynamics of Drama: Theory and Method of Analysis*. Knopf, 1970.
2. Frank, Anne. *Anne Frank: The Diary of a Young Girl*. Doubleday, 1984.
3. Marsh, James, ed. *The Canadian Encyclopedia*. Hurtig Publishers, 1985.
4. Garrigue, Sheila. *The Eternal Spring of Mr. Ito*. Bradbury, 1985.
5. Kogawa, Joy. *Naomi's Road*. Oxford University Press, 1986.
6. Kogawa, Joy. *Obasan*. Penguin, 1983.
7. Uchida, Yoshiko. *Journey Home*. Macmillan, 1982.
8. Takashima, Shizuye. *A Child in Prison Camp*. Tundra Books, 1971.
9. Robinson, Lee Bolton. Unpublished Notes.

. . . .

TEACHING DRAMATICALLY

Teaching in Role

Dramatic playing offers teachers a wide choice of teaching strategies. Teaching in role is probably the most effective way to engage the students' interest, maintain a clear focus for their work, and help them to approach material in new and interesting ways.

Teaching in role is also the most challenging of all the strategies for a teacher to use in dramatic playing, and the most likely to be misunderstood and misused. However, mastery of the skills required to work in role should help the teacher become proficient in the use of other drama teaching strategies for the simple reason that teaching in role is primarily concerned with teaching and not with acting.

CHIEF CHARACTERISTICS OF TEACHING IN ROLE

A few years ago there was a newspaper article about the teacher in role entitled *Why Does Teacher Always Get the Best Parts?* This title, although not the content of the article, misrepresented the use of teaching in role. There may be many reasons why a teacher chooses to work in role in dramatic playing, but the one probably furthest from his or her mind is to take a starring part.

The ability to project oneself in the classroom, to know when to speak and when to remain silent, to be a skilful questioner and to know how to respond to a comment or a question and, above all, to remain alert to the unspoken word and gesture are essential to teaching in role. But then these are also the qualities we recognise in any skilful teaching.

The chief distinguishing characteristic of teaching in role is that of the attitude a teacher adopts and projects within the context of the dramatic playing, even though that attitude may be one of apparent disinterest or detached neutrality. In the neighborhood park unit, the teacher as parks' board chairman may have played the role of someone in a position of authority, but the attitude she revealed to the students was one of respect for them as professional planners as well as an enthusiasm for the projected park. It was this attitude that helped the students define the attitudes they projected in their own roles.

In her initial negotiations with the students in role, the teacher projected attitudes of "I-need-your-expertise" and "Tell-me-what-you-know." When she changed her role to that of the elderly woman in a low status position, her attitude was one of displeasure with the planners at being excluded from using the park: "I-feel-left-out; so-what-are-you-going-to-do-about-it?" Again, this attitude shaped the attitudes of the students in role as they defended the decision to create a children's park.

As the situation alters or develops as when the planners offer to find ways of helping her and other elderly people to gain admittance to the park, so may the elderly person's attitude change to one of "I-need-your-help." Therefore, in dramatic playing, it is the dramatic situation that defines the roles the teacher takes and it is the situation that shapes the attitudes that are revealed through the role-taking.

Dorothy Heathcote,[1] the brilliant and innovative drama educator whose work and writings have influenced a generation of drama teachers around the world, writes:

> Drama is anything which involves people in active role taking situations in which attitudes not characters are the chief concern. It is lived at life rate and obeys the laws of suspension of disbelief, agreeing to pretence, employing all experience and imagination available in an attempt to create a moving picture of life which aims at surprise and discovery for the participants.

Even in those situations where the teacher is not taking a fictional role in the dramatic playing, the attitude that s/he projects can confirm, question, or oppose the attitudes or stances taken by the students.

In her description of what she calls "the authentic teacher" (the capacity of a teacher to behave in an authentic way), Heathcote defines the tasks that a teacher performs both in and out of role to help students embody knowledge for themselves in contrast to being passive recipients of information. Cecily O'Neill[2] summarizes these tasks as follows:

Encouraging student interaction and decision-making.
Learning to present problems differently to students.
Establishing a context for learning.
Taking more risks with materials.
Imagining and carrying out a variety of tasks.
Giving constant attention to detail.
Engineering a greater variety of reflective techniques.
Working with focus and significance to harness students' needs.
Tolerating ambiguity.
Devising fruitful encounters between self, students, ideas, knowledge, and skills.
Engendering productive tension.
Giving power to students.
Working to bring schools and society together.

NEGOTIATING IN ROLE

To illustrate what Dorothy Heathcote is saying about the tasks undertaken by a teacher, and the use of teaching in role as a means of enabling children to incarnate or embody knowledge for themselves, here are three examples of teacher-student negotiations in role.

In all three examples, the English drama educator Gavin Bolton is working with a mixed-age class of ten- to twelve-year-old students on the subject of "A Hospital of the Future." In the dramatic playing, the teacher and students are exploring a situation in which the hospital administration has introduced robots into the children's ward to perform some of the duties previously performed by nurses. Parents of children who are about to be admitted to hospital are naturally concerned about the effect this innovation will have on the quality of care their children will receive.

At one point in the dramatic playing a group of parents visits the hospital to talk to the doctors and nurses about the robots. Before the doctors and nurses meet with the parents, the teacher in role as a hospital administrator talks to them about how they are going to handle the parents' questions.

Note:

TR = Teacher in Role as Hospital Administrator; SR1, SR2, SR3 = Students in Role as Medical Staff

TR: And unfortunately I understand that a reporter from the newspaper is also hovering around the hospital. And we don't want any more unfavorable reports to come our way. So before you go in and face those parents, just give me a few ideas on what you might put to them.

SR1: The fact is that there still are some nurses.

TR: Ah, yes. Yes, they probably think there's no nurses at all. That's a good point.

SR2: The nurses still do work.

SR1: The robots can't talk, and the nurses can.

TR: So the efficiency's improved.

SR3: And the robots can make the children laugh and cheer them up.

TR: Ah. Can I just check with you? Is that the line that you are going to take: that the robots are partly entertaining as well as efficient?

In introducing the threat of unfavorable publicity to the hospital in addition to warning them about their impending interviews with the parents, the teacher infuses the dramatic playing with a sense of tension and crisis. The attitude he projects is that of someone who is first and foremost anxious to preserve the good name of the hospital: "How-are-you-going-to-handle-this-problem?"

By the time the students in role as doctors and nurses meet with the parents, they will have discussed a wide range of concerns that the parents might have, and the ways in which they could answer the parents' questions. Meanwhile, the four students taking the roles of the parents each sit in one of the circles of chairs representing four waiting rooms, listening to the conversation between the teacher in role and the other students, thereby picking up clues about the different sorts of attitude that they may wish to portray in their roles.

After allowing the parent-doctor interviews to proceed for some time, the teacher re-enters the dramatic playing, this time in role as the newspaper reporter. Adopting a stance of one who is both sympathetic to the parents and suspicious of the hospital's intentions ("I'm-not-sure-I-can-really-go-along-with-this"), the teacher is able to encourage the students in role of parents to express their feelings. At the same time, he presses the students in role as doctors and nurses to address the parents' concerns, and reflect on ethical problems involving the use of robots in the hospital.

Note: TR = Teacher in Role as Reporter; SRD1 and SRD2 = Students in Role as Doctors; SRP = Student in Role as Parent

SRD1: The robots never get angry.

TR: I must say I've not thought of that. What do you think of that?

SRP: Sure, they may not get angry with the children. They may not do anything as far as "No, no, no, bad, bad, bad!" But the child is going to look at them and get, you know, a sort of torn feeling inside wondering what's going on.... You know they're used to having gentle nurses, maybe not every time gentle ... Having the robots (is) a new thing to them.

TR: Yes, what do you say to that, doctor?

SRD1: Ya, well see, also they're disguised, but they look very much like nurses.

TR: Oh, they're in disguise. Do you want the children to know that they are robots in disguise, or do you want the children to think they are nurses?

SRD2: I think they would prefer thinking they're nurses.

TR: So are you telling the children a lie?

SRD2: No, well, we don't tell a lie. We just say that it's O.K. going into the hospital.

By the end of this lesson, the teacher is able to withdraw from the dramatic playing. The negotiations are now conducted entirely by the students in a whole-class setting as those in role as parents talk about their feelings, and ask the doctors and nurses questions about the intelligence and skill of the robots, the loss of nursing positions, and the hospital treatment of their children. Finally, in response to the parents' request, the hospital mounts a demonstration in which they see the robots caring for patients in the ward.

One final example from this drama illustrates how the teacher in role need not necessarily be taking a clearly defined role such as hospital administrator or reporter, although he still retains an important teaching role in the dramatic playing. Often this allows the teacher to project a more neutral attitude in which he supports what the students say, and helps them clarify their thinking.

The drama "A Hospital of the Future" contained two stories. The first was about the hospital itself and the introduction of the robot nurses. In contrast with that story a second one emerged about a six-year-old girl who has been diagnosed as having cancer and who is soon to enter the hospital in order to have an operation.

The child, named Theresa by the students, is naturally frightened about having cancer, about entering the hospital, and also about stories of the robots. She has been having nightmares, and in order to allay her fears as much as possible, her parents talk to her. The teacher asks the class to sit in a semicircle on the floor around "Theresa's chair" on which Theresa's doll is placed. The doll was also selected by the students. The teacher asks a volunteer to take the role of the parent standing by the chair. One of the girls, Carla, quickly offers to be the parent, and moves to the chair.

In the out-of-role discussion preceding the dramatic playing the teacher guides Carla in her depiction of the role, and asks the class for their suggestions.

Note:

T = Teacher; C = Carla; I = Ian

T: All right, now Carla is standing up by the chair, Theresa's chair, and Theresa tells her she's had a bad dream.

T: As Carla looks at the child ... Are you going to do anything with Theresa as you stand there?

(C. shrugs shoulders)

T: Are you going to touch her?

(Pause)

T: What do people think?

I: Well, she could tell her to sit on her knee.

T: Ah! How do you feel about that?

(Pause)

T: Would you have Theresa on your knee?

(C. nods her head)

T: O.K. What would you do with the doll?

C: Put it on my knee with Theresa.

Painstakingly, the teacher works with Carla to create the picture of the parent listening to Theresa talking about her bad dream, while the rest of the class offer their suggestions. "Is she looking away from you as she tells you about her dream?" the teacher asks. "Looking toward me," Carla replies.

Gradually the picture emerges of the parent, sitting down with Theresa, clutching her doll, sitting on her knee. Parent and child are looking into each other's eyes, as the students, in turn, speak what they think the mother is saying to Theresa. On this occasion, the children need no prompting as they make their contributions.

The teacher stands to one side of the semicircle gathered around Theresa's chair, choruslike echoing each statement, giving their words significance. There is a slow and dignified sense of ritual to the occasion.

Note:

T = Teacher; MRM = Michael in role as Mother; GRM = Gillian in role as Mother; SR = Susan in role as Mother

MRM: It's only a dream. There's nothing to worry about. You're home now.

(T: You're home again. Home.)

GRM: The hospital's safe and nobody will hurt you there.

(T: The hospital is safe like home is safe.)

SRM: Um, you'll ... it'll seem like everybody's so nice there ... it'll seem like, um, you're not there. It'll seem like you're only there for a day.

(T: Time's going to pass very quickly there, and it'll seem like a day, this mother says.)

Up to this point, the children have been speaking in the role of Theresa's mother. When the teacher asks the children to speak to Theresa as if they were her father, he meets with some resistance from Alan.

Note:

T = Teacher; A = Alan

T: Let's have the picture again. What's this father going to say?

A: I don't know 'cause fathers don't usually go into that kind of stuff. The mothers usually talk.

T: Oh. Your six-year-old daughter cannot share her dreams with you?

A: Like, I've known people who don't talk to their fathers about things. They only talk to their mothers.

T: What kind of father do you want to be?

A: Well, I don't know. It's hard to say.

The teacher does not comment further. Other children speak in role as father to Theresa about her dream. Then, without any prompting from the teacher, Alan breaks his silence and speaks again.

A: He probably could say the robots are there to help you, not kill you.

T: Right, so you think that's what you would have said.

A: Ya.

(Pause)

A: [now in role as father again speaking to the girl] You won't turn into a frog or anything like that.

It is difficult for Alan to speak as if he is Theresa's father. Although he does not say he is too embarrassed to assume this role in the presence of his peers, he does reveal that he is entrenched in a conventional mode of thinking that will not permit a father to talk to his daughter about personal matters. In response, the teacher briefly steps out of the dramatic playing to challenge the boy's thinking.

Whether or not Alan really does change his views about father-daughter relationships as a result of this brief exchange is impossible to say. However the teacher's intervention, at this point out of role, helps Alan to reveal his present level of thinking, to voice his reflections on his thinking, and to explore an alternative way of responding to the situation.

Teacher-student negotiations lie at the heart of dramatic playing, and perform a crucial function in enabling children to assume control *of* their thinking and to recognise responsibility *for* their thinking. The fictional roles that both teacher and student assume are always subordinate to the reflective thinking that must occur in or as a result of these negotiations for a real change of understanding to take place.

Perhaps the most telling moment in the teacher-student negotiations cited here came when Alan quite spontaneously decided to move from describing what a father *might* say to actually thinking and speaking as if he *was* the father. Dorothy Heathcote[3] says that drama places decisions in the hands of the class, while the teacher acts as midwife. She writes: "Taking a moment in time, [drama] uses the experience of the participants, forcing them to confront their own actions and decisions and to go forward to a believable outcome in which they can gain satisfaction."

Dramatic Playing Across the Curriculum

The teacher has a critical role to play in the different phases of negotiation that occur both *within* and *outside* the drama so that the students are fully aware that they are fellow negotiators in a partnership concerned with establishing learning goals for themselves. Jonothan Neelands emphasizes, in *Making Sense of Drama*,[4] the dynamic nature of classrom negotiations in which the teacher consults with students at every possible stage of the drama-learning process, and matches learning materials to the particular needs and interests of the students.

In this section, each of the following plans for dramatic playing gives special attention to the teacher-student negotiations that occur within a variety of different dramatic situations. In addition, the plans are designed to illustrate a range of drama teaching strategies including teaching in role.

In contrast with the neighborhood park where dramatic playing provided the underpinnings and structures for the entire integrated unit, here drama is used to enhance specific areas of student learning such as understanding subtext, refining questioning skills, and reading a picture or photograph. Obviously any or all of these skill-related activities could be embedded in a thematic unit and do not have to be taught separately.

The plans are not prescriptive, and are only intended to serve as a model for you to develop your own teaching plans.

Primary Reading: Working from a Picture Book

LEVEL

Ages seven to nine plus

THEME

Understanding different lifestyles

TOPIC

The changing landscape in a rural community

PICTURE BOOK

Shaker Lane by Alice and Martin Provenson. Viking Kestrel, 1987

When Abigail and Priscilla Herkimer sell off small pieces of land from their rundown farm, a tightly knit, untidy settlement develops that is regarded as an eyesore by their neighbors in Foster Hollow. After the county appropriates their land for a reservoir, the residents of Shaker Lane don't fight, they just move on. What remains of the settlement becomes a neat, new subdivision.

DRAMA TEACHING STRATEGIES

Teacher and students negotiate in role.

TOPIC QUESTIONS

What do you like most about your community?
What changes have you noticed there?
What do the inhabitants of Shaker Lane value most about their
  community?

PLAN FOR THE DRAMATIC PLAYING

With the class sitting in a circle in front of her, the teacher asks the students to name some of the things they like about the street, neighborhood or town in which they live. Are there any changes they have noticed since they have lived there? She tells the class that *Shaker Lane* describes the changes that happen to a small community.

She reads the story and shows the accompanying pictures describing the community:

> The people who lived on Shaker Lane
> took things easy.
> Their yards were full of stuff —
> old dressers ...
> cars ...
> stovepipes, bales of old wire and tin cans.
> Some people would have liked to see
> Shaker Lane disappear forever.

Displaying both covers of the book which shows a picture of Shaker Lane residents standing in front of their homes staring out as if in a photograph, surrounded by cats, dogs, and chickens, the teacher asks the children to imagine that they live in Shaker Lane. She then asks them to close their eyes and think of one thing they have seen in the pictures that they own and treasure.

When they open their eyes, she talks to them as if she is a visitor to Shaker Lane.

"You people seem to have so many things. Tell me which of you owns a dog?"

Speaking to one of the children who raises a hand, the teacher says: "There are lots of dogs. How do I know which one is yours?"

"Tell me one thing about your dog that makes him special to you."

"I hear that some people don't like all these animals running around Shaker Lane. How do you feel about that? What would you say to them?"

The questions the teacher asks are pointed but open-ended, giving every opportunity for each child to speak, use their imaginations and talk about their feelings. This simple question-and-amswer activity enables both teacher and students to feel comfortable about working in role.

When the activity is over, the students work in pairs with one taking the role of visitor and the other a resident of Shaker Lane showing the visitor around the neighborhood. The visitors have heard that Shaker Lane is a mess and a disgrace to the community. Can the residents persuade them that in spite of the untidiness this is a great place to live? Are there things more important than having a neat backyard which Shaker Lane residents value? The pairs spread out through the room, with each resident taking a visitor around pointing out the sights.

When this is completed, the visitors and residents share their impressions of Shaker Lane, the people who live there, and the visitors themselves.

The teacher asks the students in role as visitors: "Is there anything you saw or found out that would make you want to go and tell people that Shaker Lane really is a great place to live?

"Given the chance, would you go and live there?"

The teacher asks the students in role as residents: "Did you think you made a good impression on the visitors?"

"If there was one memory that you would like the visitors to take away with them, what would it be?"

Further opportunities abound for exploration of the book's rich subtext using dramatic playing:

— Who *was* responsible for deciding Shaker Lane would be the site of the new reservoir and why?
— What sort of community is Foster Hollow?
— What memories of Shaker Lane do the two sisters and the former residents have of the place now that much of the land is submerged in the reservoir?
— What was one thing each member of the community took with him or her before leaving to serve as a memento of their life in Shaker Lane?
— What does Old Man Van Sloop tell the residents of Reservoir Road about the old days in Shaker Lane?

REVIEWING THE TEACHING AND LEARNING

Working with a picture book provides the class with a focus for their attention and serves as a control for the teacher, particularly if this is the first time she and the class have taken roles. Sharing a picture book is an everyday experience in many primary classrooms, and the dramatic playing described here just takes the experience one step further. In this activity, students take a role, think intuitively, express feelings, share ideas with others, and use descriptive language. The attitude that the teacher projects in her role as visitor is one of interested listener. After the pairs activity she assumes a "tell-me-what-you-found-out" attitude, at times showing surprise or doubt at their answers, pushing students to defend a position, saying, for example: "Do you mean to say you would be quite happy to live with a rusty old car in your front yard?"

RESOURCE MATERIAL

There are many excellent picture books available that can be used in dramatic playing. I chose *Shaker Lane* to serve as an example because:
The story is concerned with some universal human issues.
The pictures supplement and expand on the text.
Neither the pictures nor the text moralize; they just tell the story.

Intermediate Reading: Responding to a Novel

LEVEL

Ages nine to eleven plus

THEME

Assessing and judging character

TOPIC

Selecting crew members for a hazardous voyage

NOVEL

Mystery in the Frozen Lands by Martyn Godfrey*

BACKGROUND TO THE NOVEL

The disappearance of the British explorer Sir John Franklin and his crew in the Canadian Arctic in 1847, while charting the Arctic seaboard, precipitated numerous would-be rescue operations. At the start of this fictionalized account of one such voyage which began in 1857, Captain Leopold McClintock is about to hire a crew for a voyage to the Arctic to discover the fate of Sir John Franklin. There have been thirty-nine previous unsuccessful attempts to discover his whereabouts, but Lady Franklin, the explorer's wife, still believes her husband is alive and has commissioned this search. Franklin's twelve-year-old nephew, Peter Griffin, the ship's cabin boy on this latest rescue mission, tells the story of the voyage.

DRAMA TEACHING STRATEGIES

Teacher and students negotiate in role; teacher and students write in role.

---

* Other suitable sources: Martyn Godfrey's novel is Canadian. A number of other children's books with historical themes describing voyages to other lands could be used for the following drama with some modifications. Patricia Clapp's *Constance: A Story of Early Plymouth* is written in diary form by the main character, Constance Hopkins, and begins on the deck of the *Mayflower* in November, 1620. Paula Fox's *The Slave Dancer* tells the story of the voyage of a slave ship from the point of view of thirteen-year-old Jessie Bollier, a white boy, who is shanghaied to play his fife so the slaves will dance and keep fit. In (Wortis) Avi's *The True Confessions of Charlotte Doyle*, thirteen-year-old Charlotte who has just left her English boarding school discovers that she is the only female aboard a ship bound for Providence, Rhode Island, from Liverpool in 1832. Complete bibliographical information is given in the resource list at the end of this chapter.

How would you feel about leaving your home at your present age to go to an unknown land?
What qualities should Captain McClintock be seeking in the crew members he hires for the rescue mission?

PLAN FOR THE DRAMATIC PLAYING

The students sit in a large circle around the teacher. The teacher talks to them in role as a reporter for an English newspaper, *The Times*, giving them background information to the novel.

> I've just heard word of another attempt to discover what happened to Sir John Franklin and his crew. You will recall he and his crew disappeared about thirteen years ago trying to find a shipping route through the Northwest Passage. This will be the fortieth voyage to find out what happened. Oh, and I nearly forgot; I hear Sir John's own twelve-year-old nephew, Peter, will be cabin boy on the voyage. I wonder what he feels about going?

Out of role the teacher asks the students to form groups of three and talk about how they would feel about leaving home at their present age to go on such a dangerous mission, particularly as there had been so many unsuccessful previous attempts.

After five minutes of brainstorming ideas, the teacher resumes her role as reporter and talks to the entire class as if each of them is Peter.

> Thank you, Peter, for agreeing to talk to me. As you know *The Times* has always kept close watch on the fate of Sir John, and we are particularly interested in the fact that you, his own flesh and blood, may help to solve this mystery. Tell me, Peter, what are your feelings about leaving home to make this journey, and can you give me some sense of why you are feeling this way?

As the students create a voice collage about the prospect of leaving home, the reporter records their spoken thoughts in her notebook.

> I'm a bit afraid because other ships and their crews have gone in search of the answers, and no one has found the missing ships. What if the same thing happens to us as happened the first time to my uncle?

I'm feeling a little sad because I'm going to miss my family, and I don't know how long I'll be gone.

I'm really excited because none of my mates has had an adventure like this.

I'm pretty happy because it's an honor to be chosen to go on a voyage of discovery like this. I'm proud to go on a voyage that will finally let my family know what happened to my uncle. It's been a worry to us.

In the moments of reflection at the end of the activity, a number of students wonder aloud why a twelve-year-old boy would be allowed to go on a voyage like this. Their reflections provide the teacher with the foundation of two succeeding lessons in which the students undertake library research into life in mid-nineteenth century England including education, work expectations, children's roles, and contrasts in standards of living. In addition, an elderly local resident visits the class to answer their questions based on stories told by his grandparents who had grown up in nineteenth century England.

Through their library research, the group discussion that follows about their findings, and their conversation with the local resident, the students are encouraged to examine the socio-historical background that will be helpful to them in their understanding and appreciation of the story.

FURTHER EXPLORATION OF THE NOVEL THROUGH DRAMATIC PLAYING

Following their library research, the teacher in the role of ship's captain asks her students in role as the captain's friends to assist her in the hiring of the crew for the impending voyage. This process involves:

1. Brainstorming those special human qualities that will be needed to undertake such a hazardous journey and make the crew superior to previous crews that have failed.
2. Selecting three broad categories from their list about which prospective applicants should be questioned. The class decides to include: the qualities required of a seaman, their awareness of expected dangers, and their personal expectations.
3. Determining what should be listed under each category (students work in independent groups), and sharing and supplementing lists (students work in whole class discussion group).

4. Speaking to the captain (teacher in role) as his friends and colleagues about what qualities he should be looking for in his crew. For example, one student says: "Well, Captain, if I wanted the glory of success, I would be working especially hard to make the success a reality. So if you have a crew full of men who want glory, you're certain to be successful."
5. Writing newspaper advertisements for crew members based on their previous small group discussions.
6. Students now assume the roles as prospective candidates for the crew, and write their applications to the captain.
7. Brainstorming questions to be used by the captain in the interviews. For example, their questions include:
   What makes you think you have the qualities I am looking for?
   How do you feel about leaving your family for an indefinite period of time?
   How will you feel if we don't succeed in our mission?
   How can I be sure you won't cave in under pressure if the dangers of the voyage become too great?
8. Interviewing applicants (students work in pairs) using the questions that have been generated. In response to the final question "How can I be sure you won't cave in under pressure?" one candidate replies: "I come from a long line of noble seamen, and I have within me all the strength of my ancestors. I am a fighter."
9. After the students, now in role as friends of the captain, decide that all the applicants should be hired because they had given strong supporting statements in their answers to the questions, the reading aloud begins. At this point, the teacher allows the drama of the story itself to take over as she reads Peter's journal which starts with the entry: *November 10, 1858. Aboard the Fox, frozen in the ice off Port Kennedy, Beliot Strait.*

REVIEWING THE TEACHING AND LEARNING

In these sessions, the dramatic playing is used in conjunction with personal response journals to create a literate context for learning in which a relationship is built between the lives and experiences of the students and that of the world that they will encounter in the text of the novel. Thus, the dramatic playing takes place prior to students reading the novel. In their dramatic playing, the students are encouraged to find a purpose for reading, as well as for engaging in talk, listening, and writing, through problem-solving, making decisions, group discussion, expressing and sharing opinions, taking fresh perspectives in role, and reflection.

Susan Hynds[5] points out that readers become literate by not only perceiving themselves as readers through participation in a reading community, but also by developing their intellectual and social competencies for bringing what they know about life into the text. This ongoing process of bringing ''life to literature and literature to life'' is related to the likelihood of students continuing to read beyond their formal schooling years.

This novel is written in first person narrative through the use of Peter Griffin's own journal, and therefore opens up all sorts of possibilities for the students' own writing in role. Because the novel is set in the past, dramatic playing can also help the students gain a greater sense of the historical context in which the story takes place.

Social Studies: Interpreting a Photograph

LEVEL

Ages twelve to fourteen plus

THEME

Understanding peoples' lives in other times

TOPIC

Migration from and within the prairie provinces during the Depression years

PHOTOGRAPH

Black and white photograph showing a family on the journey from their farm to seek better land from *The Hungry Thirties: 1930-1940* by Max Braithwaite*

---

* Other suitable sources: Although the source for this dramatic playing is Canadian, many illustrated history books contain photographs that you could use as a basis for a still image. For example, James D. Horan's *The Great American West* has pictures of early settlers on the American prairies. 2D Publications in the United Kingdom have published a number of resource packs that include vivid black and white photographs and suggestions for use in dramatic playing. One set deals with the American West. For Australian photographs of early settlers, try R.M. Younger's *Australia, Australia: March to Nationhood* or John Larkins' and Bruce Howard's *The Great Australia Book of Nostalgia*. Complete bibliographical information is given in the resource list at the end of this chapter.

In the 1930s, the world wide economic depression and drought-related crop failures drove many farm families from the Canadian prairie provinces. This photograph shows a family of five standing in front of their horse drawn cart and staring grimly at the photographer. The two boys, (aged about five and eight) stand on either side of their father. Their mother, holding a baby, stands to one side; she appears to be pregnant. Father wears coveralls and a cap; the two boys are in work clothes; mother wears an ill-fitting coat and the baby wears woollen clothes. Behind them in the open section of the cart is a Holstein milk cow, while the front section is covered in patched tarpaulin and paper sacking.

DRAMA TEACHING STRATEGIES

Taking a role; creating a still image.

TOPIC QUESTIONS

What would drive a family to leave their land and seek a new life elsewhere?
What hopes and expectations do they have for the future?

PLAN FOR THE DRAMATIC PLAYING

For this lesson, which is part of an ongoing thematic unit about immigration and migration, the teacher has prepared an overhead projector copy of the photograph. The students have already conducted some research into the topic of the Depression in Canada during the 1930s. They are now seated in a circle around the screen with an empty space in the middle of the room.

The teacher says: "This photograph was taken on the prairies during the early years of the Depression. Just by looking at the family, what could you say about them?"

The students offer a number of suggestions:

"They look sad."

"They're poor."

"Everything they have is on the wagon."

"The smaller kid's clothes are too big. He's wearing his brother's old clothes."

"They look tired. They have been on the road a long time."

"They're going to look for new farm. That's why they're taking the cow."

"It's a heavy load for the horse to pull. Why doesn't the cow walk?"

Teacher: That's an interesting question. In fact you have raised a number of questions about the family in the picture. Are they as unhappy and poor as they seem to be? Do they know where they are going? What will happen to them when they get there? Let's take a moment to think of some of the things that we could ask the family if we could have them right here. Take some time also to think about the family itself. The mother is holding the baby. I wonder if the father or the boys ever look after the baby? I also wonder who milks the cow while they are on the journey?

The teacher asks the class to work in groups of three to brainstorm five questions, with one of the group writing down the questions.

After five minutes the groups share their questions with the rest of the class. The teacher writes them on the board. Questions include:

Where have you come from and where are you going?
Why are you making this journey?
Was the baby born before or after you left?
Why are you taking the cow and why is it riding on the cart?
Why are you using a horse and cart? Don't you have a tractor?
Where do you go to school? (to the older boy)

When each group has read out its questions the teacher asks the class: "If you could speak to one of the people in this picture, which person would you choose? The father, mother, or one of the two boys?"

By a show of hands, the students decide to talk to the elder son. The teacher invites any one in the class to take the role of the boy.

Teacher: Anyone can take the role. When you stand up, think about the way the boy in the picture is standing. What thoughts could be running through his head as he stares at the camera. When you are asked a question, answer as truthfully as possible as if you were the boy. If you can't answer a question just say you don't know. Perhaps we shall have to bring other members of the family into the picture to help you answer the question.

A girl volunteers to take the role of the son, and stands in the centre of the room, hands thrust down and her head down like the boy in the picture. The teacher asks the class to study the portrayal quietly, compare it with the picture, and offer any suggestions that might help the student.

"The boy's shoulders are sort of hunched," one student says.

"He's screwing up his eyes looking into the sun."

The girl follows their directions and alters her stance and facial expression. After a few suggestions, the teacher says:

"It is late in the year 1935. After months without rain on the prairies, many farm families are so desperate after another year of crop failures that they abandon their farms and set out to seek a life elsewhere. Behind them the rich soil that their family farmed for over thirty years has turned to dust. One such family packs all its belongings, including the milk cow, onto a cart, and leaves their farm to seek a new life elsewhere."

Turning to the girl taking the role of the son, the teacher quietly asks: "Would you please tell us your name?"

The girl replies, "Ben. My dad is called Ben, too."

"Can you tell us where you came from, Ben?" the teacher inquires.

"Moose Jaw, Saskatchewan. That's where our farm was. I was born there."

"Is there anyone who would like to talk to Ben?" The teacher turns to the class.

"Where are you going?" one student asks.

"Penticton, British Columbia. My uncle has an orchard there."

The class asks a number of questions. When the girl in role cannot answer one question, the mother is added to the picture and then the father. Different students assume the roles of the members of the family. When a student in role has difficulties in answering a question, the teacher asks the whole class for suggestions of what s/he might say. For the most part the students playing the family are able to answer the questions knowledgeably because they have already done some research on the topic. The father, therefore, can say that his tractor was taken from him because he still owed money on it. Occasionally there are difficulties in role. No one is quite sure whether or not there was television in 1935. That is something that can be checked later, and does not interfere with the students' belief in the dramatic playing.

Finally, the teacher asks the whole class to imagine that they are the elder son Ben five years later at the age of thirteen (the average age of this class), looking at the photograph and remembering that moment in his life. The teacher asks them to speak as if each one of them is Ben, and to say one thing they can remember about the journey.

In their journals, the students write a short account of the journey in first person narrative either as Ben, his brother, his father, or mother.

FURTHER EXPLORATION OF THE TOPIC THROUGH DRAMATIC PLAYING

The class traces the events that led to Ben's family having to leave the farm. Working in groups of five, the students create still images that show the different misfortunes they think may have contributed to the family's departure. The still images include the family huddled in the farmhouse during a dust storm, reseeding and cleaning up after a dust storm, pleading with an implement supplier not to take back the tractor, the family fruitlessly attempting to drive away swarms of grasshoppers which are about to eat their crops, the death of the boy's elder sister in a blizzard. As each still image is shown the teacher uses a number of different strategies to explore different levels of meaning contained in the scene. The strategies include:

1. Asking the class to look at the still image and suggest a caption for the picture.
2. Asking the class to study the still image carefully and say how it tells them more about the family in terms of their individual personal qualities and characteristics, their relationships with one another, and the hardships they had to face.
3. Asking the class to choose one person in the still image whom they would like to question, and bringing that person out of the picture.
4. Asking the class to describe in brief phrases the feelings that the still image projects.
5. Asking the students who created the still image to bring the picture to life and show what happened immediately after the event they are depicting. This is done silently in slow motion and then frozen again. Each character in the still image now briefly speaks his or her thoughts.

As an extension, the students could look at Canadian paintings of this period or later ones that depict life on the prairies during the Depression, for example those by William Kurelek.

The class could also compare the migration of the people in the Depression with that of contemporary refugees and immigrants, as well as with those who immigrated to the Canadian prairies in the early part of the century.

REVIEWING THE TEACHING AND LEARNING

Photographs, particularly black and white ones, can provide many opportunities for dramatic playing. Here the teacher uses the picture as a means of enabling the students to identify with the plight of the family, and to study the events that preceded the scene represented in the photo. Because this is a photograph, (and also because it was taken over fifty years ago), the students can look at it with a certain level of detachment and objectivity. At the same time, the recreation of the picture provides an opportunity for the class to explore human relationships at a very personal level. The teacher has used the still image in these dramatic playing sessions to place the students in a dramatic situation where they are negotiating in role with one another, asking questions, and creating their own still images. The attitude the teacher is projecting to the class is one of "interested listener and observer." Throughout the sessions, the teacher is seeking ways to deepen the students' level of understanding and show them different and interesting ways of exploring the theme and topic dramatically. With constructive and imaginative support from the teacher, the students taking the roles of the different members of the family are able to handle questions with confidence and sincerity.

RESOURCE MATERIALS

In addition to photographs, freeze frames on videos, advertisements, posters, record album covers, paintings, sculptures, and murals can provide excellent sources of material for still images. Also, letters, memorabilia, pamphlets, and stories from old newspapers can all be used as ways to start dramatic playing as well as forming an integral part of the playing itself.

Exploring a Fairy Tale

LEVEL

Ages six to eleven

THEME

Considering and making choices in one's life

TOPIC

Examining the princess's motives for rewarding Taro in the way she did for the kindness he showed her.

FAIRY TALE

"Urashima Taro or the Tale of Taro from Urashima" in *A World of Stories*, folktales collected and retold by Andrea Spalding; *Urashima Taro* by Robert B. Gordman and Robert A. Spicer; *Urashima Taro and Other Stories* by Florence Sakade.

BACKGROUND TO THE FAIRY TALE

Taro, a young fisherman, lives with his mother in the village of Urashima. One day, on the beach, he exchanges his small catch for a little turtle that the children plan to make into turtle soup. When he releases the turtle, the creature is transformed into Otohime, daughter of the Sea Dragon. She invites Taro back to her palace beneath the sea. After ten days Taro returns home with a box from Otohime, and a warning not to open the box unless he wishes to return to her. The story ends sadly when Taro realises he has been away for one hundred years. When he clumsily opens the box he is transformed into a very old man.
Note: In the story the time span is one thousand years. I have changed it so that there may just be an elderly resident who was born before Taro's mother died.

DRAMA TEACHING STRATEGIES

Negotiating in role; hot seating; overheard conversations.

TOPIC QUESTIONS

If the princess was so grateful to Taro, why didn't she tell him what would happen if he visited the undersea palace?
Did Taro ever think of the consequences of his decision to accompany the princess?

As part of a thematic unit dealing with contrasting lifestyles and values in contemporary Japan, the teacher has just read her class the story of Urashima Taro. Because the story is very different from the sort of fairy tales or folk tales written in a European, North American, or Australian tradition with which her ten-year-old students are familiar, the teacher has decided to use dramatic playing to explore those aspects of the story that are difficult for her class to understand.

In the previous lesson the teacher has asked the class to think of any questions they might have about the story. Their questions include:

> Why didn't the princess tell Taro he would never see his mother again if he went with her?
> Why did Taro leave his mother without even telling her where he was going?
> Once he was in the palace, why didn't he ask to send for his mother, or send a message to her saying he was all right?
> If the princess really cared about Taro and wanted him to return, why didn't she just become a turtle again?
> What was the purpose of tying the box in a golden thread?

As most of the questions appear to concern the princess's actions, the teacher, out of role, decides to use her as the central figure in the dramatic playing.

Teacher: Many of the questions you are asking are concerned with the princess and the way she mistreated Taro. Remember she told Taro that the Sea Dragon commanded her to bring him back. I thought it might be interesting to explore what happened when the Sea Dragon told her she had to return with Taro. Perhaps he had a reason for wanting Taro in the palace, and was able to convince his daughter not to tell Taro the truth. Let's first discover what happened during their conversation after Otohime had been saved by Taro.

In pairs the students recreate the meeting of the Sea Dragon with Otohime up to the moment when the princess decides to return with Taro. After five minutes, the teacher stops the dramatic play.

Teacher: Let's imagine the end of the story is different, and that

Taro is able to return to the palace of the Sea Dragon after his discovery that one hundred years have passed since he left. How would Taro feel now that he had lost his mother and been cheated out of his life on land? What would he say to Princess Otohime about the way she had behaved?

The class sits on chairs in a large circle. The teacher sits in the middle of the circle facing an empty chair. A small laquered box is placed on the chair, signifying the fact that this is where Taro is sitting. The teacher takes the role of the princess and is "hot seated" by the class who role play Taro's voice trying to find out why Otohime had not told him the whole truth.

Taro: Why didn't you tell me that I would never see my mother again?
Princess: Because when I invited you to visit the palace you never even mentioned your mother. I naturally assumed that she was of no further concern to you.
Taro: You didn't invite me. You said I was commanded to come by the Sea Dragon!
Princess: Do you always do what you are told to do?

The intense cross examination continues until the teacher in role as princess suggests to the class that they replay excerpts from the conversation between the Sea Dragon and Otohime. Going back to their original pairs, the students select one moment from their dialogue that might help Taro to understand why he was not told what would happen if he accompanied the princess to the palace. In sequence, the pairs present these snatches of dialogue.

FURTHER EXPLORATION OF THE TOPIC THROUGH DRAMATIC PLAYING

1. Creating a sequel to the story in which Taro confronts the Sea Dragon, demanding that he be returned to his own time. Will the Sea Dragon agree, and what will he ask in return for this favor?
2. The teacher in role as Taro's mother asks the villagers to help her secure the release of her son. The crashing waves have told her that he is held captive in the Sea Dragon's palace.

REVIEWING THE TEACHING AND LEARNING

Fairy tales, folk tales, and myth offer many opportunities for dramatic playing because they are concerned with age-old, universal human issues and problems. At the same time, they often pose more questions than they answer. (For example, exactly what did the peddler say to Jack that would persuade him to part with the money he had just received for selling the family cow in exchange for a handful of beans?) By asking the class to identify those questions they have about the story of Taro, the teacher is giving the initial focus for the dramatic playing. The pairs' work at the start of the session provides the students with the background that they will need in their roles as Taro. In addition, by asking the students to assume the roles of the Sea Dragon, Otohime, and Taro, the teacher is giving them an opportunity to look at the same issue from a number of differing perspectives.

Both the language they use and the attitudes they assume in each dramatic situation will vary according to the context (Sea Dragon ordering his daughter to return with Taro; Taro demanding an explanation from Otohime); the roles they take; and the group setting (the informal setting of pairs work compared with the whole class setting, which is more like a formal performance). In role as Otohime, the teacher projects an attitude that continually challenges the students' questions, in role as Taro. This requires them to reflect on the choices and decisions that Taro made by trusting the princess.

Like the picture book, the novel, and the photograph in the previous dramatic playing sessions, there is a story behind the story just waiting to be discovered in this fairy tale. Dramatic playing helps children deal with those age-old questions of ''I wonder what happened then?''; ''I wonder why he did that?'', and ''There must be something that happened before the story began that we were never told about. I wonder what it was?''

Dramatic playing can help create imagined realities out of those wonderings. If the children are not satisfied with their dramatizations, then of course they can try again. There are many children who listen to the story of *Urashima Taro* and say ''I wish it had had a happy ending.'' Teachers who use dramatic playing, can reply, ''What sort of happy ending would you like the story to have?'' knowing that the children can test their ideas dramatically. However, there are no guarantees that their ending will either be as satisfying or as fitting as the original one. Children will have to draw their own conclusions about that.

REFERENCES CITED

1. Heathcote, Dorothy. "Subject or System?" In *Dorothy Heathcote: Collected Writings on Education and Drama*. Edited by Liz Johnson and Cecily O'Neill. Hutchinson, 1984.
2. O'Neill, Cecily. "Dialogue and Drama: The Transformation of Events, Ideas and Teachers." *Language Arts*. 66.5 (1989): pp. 528-539.
3. Heathcote, Dorothy. "Drama and Learning". In *Dorothy Heathcote: Collected Writings on Education and Drama*. Edited by Liz Johnson and Cecily O'Neill. Hutchinson, 1984.
4. Neelands, Jonothan. *Making Sense of Drama*. Heinemann, 1984.
5. Hynds, Susan. "Reading as a Social Event." In *Beyond Communication*. Edited by D. Bogdan and S.B. Straw. Boynton/Cook Publishers, 1990.

RESOURCE LIST

Avi, Wortis. *The True Confessions of Charlotte Doyle*. Orchard, 1990.
Braithwaite, Max. *The Hungry Thirties: 1930/1940*. N.S.L., Natural Science of Canada, 1977.
Clapp, Patricia C. *Constance: A Story of Early Plymouth*. Penguin, 1986.
Fox, Paula. *The Slave Dancer*. Bradbury, 1973.
Godfrey, Martyn. *Mystery in the Frozen Lands*. James Lorimer, 1988.
Gordman, Robert B., and Robert A. Spicer. *Urashima Taro*. Island Heritage, 1973.
Horan, James D. *The Great American West*. Crown Publishers, 1978.
_____. *Indians and Pioneers*. 2D Publications, 1986.
Larkins, John, and Bruce Howard. *The Great Australia Book of Nostalgia*. Rigby, 1975.
Sakade, Florence. *Urashima Taro and Other Stories*. C.E. Tuttle, 1958.
"Urashima Taro or the Tale of Taro from Urashima" in *A World of Stories*. Folktales collected and retold by Andrea Spalding. Red Deer College Press, 1989.
Younger, R.M. *Australia, Australia: March to Nationhood*. Rigby, 1977.

THINKING DRAMATICALLY

Teaching, Learning, and Assessment

This chapter is concerned with the assessment of learning in dramatic playing, and more specifically with some of the tools that you can use to gain a greater understanding of the different kinds of learning that have occurred. In each case, I emphasize the close relationship that exists between teaching, learning, and assessment. The examples used in this chapter are largely based on the dramatic sessions described previously.

Questioning as a Tool for Teaching and Assessment

Of the many evaluations of my teaching that I have received from both adults and children, the one I value most came from a nine-year-old student who wrote: "Thank you for coming to teach us. You asked difficult questions and made us think *hard.*"

At the beginning of this book I listed different areas of learning that can occur during dramatic playing, and stated that no one area of learning is more important than another. However, it is equally true to say that thinking in its many different forms and aspects is central to all learning. In dramatic playing the teacher is concerned not so much with what students think and what they learn, but more with the process of how they think and how they learn.

The student who projects the thought "Who will feed the ducks when I'm gone?" onto the elderly woman (page 45) has caught the despair and resignation of defeat, and the apparent inadequacy of the planners' attempt to reassure her that they will find a solution to her problem. The teacher who is concerned with the thinking processes that led to these spoken thoughts and images will find an opportunity to talk about them with her students: "It seems as if the elderly woman doesn't think she will ever return to the park. I wonder what happened during your talk with her that made her think like this?"

Therefore, in order for you to understand and assess the learning that may have occurred during dramatic playing, you need to be concerned with the thinking behind the learning. There has been a number of examples in the various dramatic playing sessions I have described where students are asked to reflect on the thinking that led them either to act or speak in a certain way.

In *Urashima Taro*, for instance, in response to the student's reply "You didn't invite me. You said I was commanded to come by the Sea Dragon!" the teacher in role as princess challenges the student to reflect about what she has just said by asking "Do you always do what you are told to do?" (page 104) Of course, the student is in role as Taro at that moment, and so ostensibly is being asked to consider whether Taro always does what he is told to do.

In this example, the question was asked during the dramatic playing negotiations in role. On other occasions the question might be asked out of role during a discussion either during or following a dramatic playing session. On all occasions, the teacher should project the attitude of someone who is genuinely seeking information and not merely trying to check whether a student is able to give the answer the teacher is expecting. In dramatic playing, the best teacher questions are those to which the teacher really does not already know the answer.

Therefore, teacher- and student-questions both in and out of role are an important element, not only of the dramatic playing itself, but also of the ongoing assessment of the learning that occurs within the dramatic playing process. At this informal level of assessment, the teacher can discover a great deal about the learning that occurred in all five areas of learning.

For example, in the intellectual area of learning a question such as "I wonder what series of events led the family to make the decision to leave their farm?" focuses on thinking about sequencing. In the emotional area of learning, the question to a visitor to Shaker Lane "What makes you feel so angry about the Shaker Lane neighborhood?" focuses on formulating and being aware of personal beliefs, attitudes, and values.

When the student in role as visitor to Shaker Lane responds

to that question he might be expressing emotions, personal beliefs, values, and attitudes different from those he personally holds. Here the teacher could ask the student to compare the answer given in role with the one that might have been given if he really had been visiting a neighborhood similar to Shaker Lane. The question in itself might help the student become aware that these differences between reality and drama playing do exist.

To assess social learning, the question "How will each group present its section of the plan to the mayor?" (page 39) focuses specifically on understanding how a group functions, although other key elements of social learning such as sharing ideas with others and being aware of and respecting other points of view are also involved in answering the question. The answer itself can help the teacher to assess to what extent her students' knowledge and understanding of group dynamics has developed since they first started their work on the neighborhood park integrated unit.

To assess drama learning, the question might be "How can we show the differences between life in Shaker Lane before the reservoir, and life in Reservoir Road after Shaker Lane had disappeared?" To answer this question students need to have some knowledge, understanding, and appreciation of ways in which drama can convey meaning, including the use of contrast, understanding the significance of sign and symbol, and being aware of the use of space, sight, and sound.

In response to this question, the class might suggest contrasting the two neighborhoods through a series of short scenes that juxtapose the cluttered, crisis-filled lifestyles of Shaker Lane with that of the neat, orderly lives of the people of Reservoir Road. This idea reveals that the class has some sense of the way in which meaning can be conveyed through the use of the dramatic art form, as well as informing the teacher that the class has understood one of the central themes of the book.

In the area of language learning, the question "What sort of questions should Captain McClintock ask of the seamen who wish to sail with him?" (page 95) focuses on questioning skills and on register, that is, the sort of language the Captain uses in an interview situation.

The range and quality of the questions asked can help the teacher assess a student's skill in asking questions. For example, in role of Captain McClintock, the student not only asks a question but has to listen carefully to the response to that question, to probe and question further into a sailor's background or experience.

Different Types of Questions in Dramatic Playing

Exploring a theme through dramatic playing offers both teacher and students many opportunities to ask questions in their negotiations with one another. Questions will vary from the simple information seeking question, "Are you the king in disguise?", to ones that require choices to be made, "Shall we take the road that goes direct to the castle or approach it from the river?"

Other questions invite comparisons such as "What similarities can you see between these two brothers?" while others require critical thinking and evaluation, "Do you think she is to be trusted?"

In most role-taking situations, the drama starts with information-seeking questions and those that require a description, "Tell me about the house where you live." As the drama develops and students feel more sure of themselves in role, their questions should become more probing and complex.

Here is a classification[1] of the different types of questions that can occur in dramatic playing:

Description

Questions involving description seek information about the given attributes of a scene or situation, and its parts (people, things, actions, thoughts and attitudes, and their relationships). They help to establish the who, what, and where of a dramatic context.

Note: T/SR = Teacher or student in role

Examples

T/SR: How long have you known this man?

T/SR: What experience have you got as a ship's cook?

T/SR: Describe the route we should be taking.

Sequence

Sequence questions reflect processes, procedures, or routines. They ask: What happens next? What is the plot?

Examples

T/SR: How will we know when we have reached the place where Franklin disappeared?

T/SR: What duties will I be expected to perform as ship's doctor?

T/SR: After I have swabbed down the deck, what should I do next?

Choice
Questions concerning choice seek answers involving alternative courses of actions, their consequences, and the decisions needed. They ask: What's the problem? What can be done? What are the consequences? How do you feel about the alternatives? What should be done?

Examples

T/SR: How do you feel about leaving your family for an indefinite period of time?

T/SR: So how do you want to be remembered — as heroes or cowards?

Moving beyond the actual construction of the imaginary world in which the participants take roles and assume ownership of the dramatic context, students are required to draw on their own background experience, knowledge, understandings and feelings to make sense of the concepts that are being explored through the medium of dramatic playing. This means they must see links between the imaginary world and the world in which they live. The type of questions that can help to achieve this level of thinking include the following.

Classification
Classification questions concern the grouping of concepts in some way. They ask: What kind, type, or sort?

Examples

T/SR: What are some of the qualities a crew member should have?

T/SR: How would you compare this ship with the last one you sailed on?

T/SR: What are some of the things that an officer can do that an ordinary seaman can't?

Projection

Projection questions are concerned with predicting, drawing conclusions, and formulating, testing, and establishing hypotheses. They ask: What might happen if...? What have you deduced? What are your reasons for thinking this way?

Examples

T/SR: How will you feel if we don't succeed in our mission?

T/SR: How can I be sure you won't cave in under pressure if the dangers and stresses of the voyage become too great?

T/SR: What is your theory about Sir John's disappearance? I understand you still think he is alive.

T/SR: What makes you think you have the qualities I am looking for?

Evaluation

Evaluation questions involve the giving of an opinion or rating. They ask: What are our chances? Which do you like?

Examples

T/SR: Are you giving honest answers, or have you been told by the captain to lie?

T/SR: So tell me: Who should I hire from this group of men?

T/SR: If you were a betting man, how would you rate our likelihood of finding Sir John?

Reflective Writing

Writing is another powerful tool for helping students to reflect on the dramatic playing. Writing provides useful feedback to the teacher about the student's present level of understanding and commitment to work. (However, note that writing is an integral component of the dramatic playing itself, and is not used exclusively as an instrument for assessment.)

The writing activities that can flow out of a dramatic situation help to build and sustain the students' belief in the work, as well as giving them an opportunity to reflect on the dramatic playing.

These include:

Diary and journal entries
Letters
Memoirs
Newspaper reports
Lists
Advertisements
Travelogues
Interview reports
Case studies
Evaluations
Captions
Questionnaires
Biographical profiles

When students are writing in role within a dramatic context they have a purpose in writing, and they have an audience for their writing other than themselves or the teacher. To give you some sense of the range and quality of the writing that can occur in dramatic playing, here are some examples drawn from a class exploring the drama involving Martyn Godfrey's *Mystery in the Frozen Lands* outlined earlier.

After each set of examples I have included a short analysis of the writing to show how student writing may be interpreted and assessed in terms of the dramatic playing. I have purposely not discussed the writing either in terms of the writing process itself or the individual writing abilities of the students.

PERSONAL DIARY WRITING

In the example that follows, the students in role of Peter write in their diaries their thoughts about the prospect of leaving home to sail with Captain McClintock.

A. I'm a bit afraid because other ships and their crews have gone in search of the answers, and no one has found the missing ships. What if the same thing happens to us as happened the first time to my uncle?
B. I'm feeling a little sad because I'm going to miss my family, and I don't know how long I'll be gone.
C. I'm really excited because none of my mates has had an adventure like this.

D. I'm pretty happy because it's an honor to be chosen to go on a voyage of discovery like this.

E. I'm proud to go on a voyage that will finally let my family know what happened to my uncle. It's been a worry to us.

ANALYSIS

At this early stage in the drama, the students are representing Peter's thoughts and feelings, but they may also be expressing their own personal views about leaving home. The oral discussion and role-taking preceding the writing have given all the students something to write about. This brief writing activity serves to synthesize what has happened thus far, to deepen the students' belief in the dramatic playing, and to provide a link to the next stage in their work.

While most of the students express a sense of apprehension, **A.** is quite specific, comparing what has already happened on previous expeditions with what might happen on the impending voyage. In the role of Peter, he also talks about Peter's uncle, John Franklin. **B.**'s writing is concerned purely with family, while **C.** regards the whole enterprise as an adventure. Both **D.** and **E.** regard their inclusion in the crew as a personal honor, although **E.** also reveals that he is concerned about the family's worry about Franklin's disappearance.

COMPILING LISTS

The teacher in role as ship's captain asks her students in role as the captain's friends to assist her in the hiring of the crew for the impending voyage. This process involves selecting three broad subjects about which prospective applicants should be questioned. The class decides to include: the qualities required of a seaman, their awareness of expected dangers, and their personal expectations. Working in small groups of three, the students classify lists of topics under each subject heading.

Group A

Qualities	Dangers	Expectations
strong	polar bears	success
wits	icebergs	find the NW
determination	frozen in	passage
education	starvation	glory
experience	diseases	adventure

Qualities	Dangers	Expectations
endurance	wild animals	money for poor
good health	getting lost	starving family
age	mutiny	friendships
hunting skills	cold	to learn
to appreciate	sinking	frostbite
things		
cooking abilities		
teamwork		
being able to hunt		

Group B

Qualities	Dangers	Expectations
hard work	starvation	learn discipline
dedicated	scurvy	respect
interested	sinking	adventure
quick thinker	animals	discover a mystery
anticipation	frostbite	glory
quick learner	suicide	new friends
seamanship	insanity	seamanship
helpful	mutiny	
patient	stuck in pack ice	
endurance		

Group C

Qualities	Dangers	Expectations
strong	getting stuck	adventures
healthy	dogs escaping	danger
ready for danger	starvation	dying
face the cold	scurvy, etc.	getting lost
ready to act	icebergs	learning
	lack of food	glory
	freezing to death	

ANALYSIS

The three lists range from the lengthy one created by Group A to the shorter list of Group C. However, many of the items listed are common to all three lists, and Group C included some useful phrases that were more specific than those supplied by the other two groups. All lists reflect the research undertaken by each group and the knowledge they have acquired about the topic. Again, the writing plays an important role in the dramatic playing, enabling the students to synthesize their research, pool their ideas, and prepare them for the roles they will take in the next activity.

WRITING ADVERTISEMENTS

Students design and write "wanted" advertisements based on their lists and small group discussions. Group B's advertisement reads:

> WANTED
>
> Officers and crew to travel on a history-making voyage to discover the fate of Sir John Frankin, a noble seaman, and his 129 seamen, lost while searching for a passage through the Arctic over the Americas.
>
> Applicants must be:
> Hard workers, dedicated, quick thinkers, patient, have endurance
> Alert to dangers:
> Scurvy, insanity, starvation, frostbite, getting stuck in pack ice
> Hopeful of:
> Money, glory, gain respect, solving a mystery, making friends

ANALYSIS

Writing the advertisements allows each group to select items on their original lists that they feel would attract the sort of crew necessary to man the ship for a dangerous voyage. Therefore, the advertisement is composed for a specific purpose and with a particular audience in mind.

Group B has chosen to leave out "mutiny" from their original list of dangers, a wise decision. Presumably, in an attempt to entice would-be crew members, they have also opted to leave out the prospect of "learning discipline!"

DRAFTING A RÉSUMÉ

Students assume the roles as prospective candidates for the crew and write their résumés for the captain. In preparation for this activity, the teacher and students have worked together to produce a form for everyone to fill in. Here are some completed examples:

Applicant A
Name: Sir Robin Robert of Wales

Position requested: Ship's Officer
Experience: My experience is six years in the Royal Navy aboard H.M.S. *Orkeney* as a first mate.
Reason for applying: I'm applying for adventure to learn friendships. I look forward finally to finding out what happened to the Franklin expedition.
I should be chosen for this expedition because of: my experience as a naval officer, my strength, and endurance. I also graduated from Oxford University with flying colors. I have many skills like navigation and all sorts of other crewman and officer skills.

Applicant B
Name: Jocohamu Coope
Position requested: Doctor
Experience: I was the doctor on the fourth expedition to find Sir John Franklin and his crew.
Reason for applying: I need the money. I want discipline to discover the mistery of the two ships.
I should be chosen for this expedition because: I have discipline and respect for my athoraties and I want to make new friends.

Applicant C
Name: Ted Norton
Position requested: Normal seaman
Experience: I know how to map land and hunt any wild animal.
Reason for applying: Need a job and some adventure.
I should be chosen for this expedition because: I want the adventure and I think the ship would need my help as a crew member.

ANALYSIS

Each of the three résumés adds more to the roles the students are creating, and to the drama itself. Applicant A has provided some clear reasons why he should be chosen to be an officer. He has officer experience, has navigation skills, and has a first-class university degree. There is a note of bravado in his résumé. The doctor, Applicant B, brings his previous experience on the fourth mission to discover Franklin to this expedition, and Applicant C.'s résumé is terse but to the point. He sounds like a practical, hardworking man. Notice how the writing seems to reflect the characters and qualities of the roles the students are taking, although Applicant B. has made no specific mention of his medical experience. It is hard to say whether it was the intention of the writers actually to sound as if they are the characters they are portraying. However, what is most important as far as the drama is concerned is that both A and C appear to believe in their roles. Applicant B probably needs to clarify his/her role further.

JOURNAL WRITING IN ROLE

During the voyage, the students in role as the ship's crew suffer many hardships but eventually discover the bodies of Franklin and his companions. Throughout the voyage, the students record these events and their thoughts and feelings in their journals. On one occasion, students speculate what the cabin boy Peter might have been feeling as the expedition starts to solve the mystery of his uncle's disappearance. They write as if they are Peter: Here is an example:

> When Anton and I were being chased by the bear I felt so terrified. When the dogs came to our rescue, though, I felt a feeling of great joy ... it was a great feeling. I know I'm right about the mystery of my uncle if only Captain McClintock could feel the same way. I never really thought about it but someday I'll have to say goodbye to Anton. During the trip I've really grown to like Anton, and he is my best friend. On the day I left from England I was only a boy but now part of me is different, I'm a man. I hope we uncover the mystery of my uncle, and my father would be proud of me. This trip has been the best experience of my life, and I don't think I'll ever experience anything like it again. In the spring journey I know we are going to find my uncle and his crew alive and well.

ANALYSIS

Through the experience of the drama, this student is able to identify very closely with Peter and his friendship with Anton. There is a sense of freshness and immediacy to the writing that the events are happening now. There are also many insights into character — "if only Captain McClintock could feel the same way" and "On the day I left England I was only a boy but now some part of me is different, I'm a man." Even though the student knows from the book that Franklin is found, in the role of Peter s/he still manages to convey the feeling that this event has not yet happened, and it is the hope of solving this mystery that sustains Peter.

WRITING NEWSPAPER REPORTS

When the expedition returns to England, students in role as newspaper reporters interview members of the crew, and write their stories. Here are two of those reports:

Reporter A

FRANKLIN MYSTERY SOLVED

On September 17, 1859, the fortieth expedition to attempt to discover the fate of John Franklin returned home with the mystery solved. "I am relieved, yet disappointed," says Peter Griffin, Franklin's nephew. "I had some hope that he was still alive." Peter and an Inuit friend, Anton, who helped with the dogs on the *Fox*, discovered the answer to the mystery themselves. They found a message in a cairn on King William Island containing the date Franklin died. All of England will be shattered by the news.

Reporter B

SIR JOHN IS DEAD!

The voyagers of the ship, the *Fox*, returned this week knowing for sure that Sir John Franklin, a noble seaman searching for the Northwest Passage over the Americas, is dead. The cabin boy who is Franklin's nephew, and an Inuit, Anton, found relics of the man and his officers and a note telling that he and his crew had died. They found many things such as cutlery and a lightning rod. Many of the items were useless and this puzzles a lot of people. Captain McClintock was the leader of the voyage. Sir John and his crew have been lost for 12 years and the *Fox* was the 40th expedition to look for Sir John Franklin. Now the mystery is solved.

ANALYSIS

The newspaper report is the climax to this drama. Although the second report certainly includes far more detail concerning the expedition, there is a greater sense of immediacy to the one written by reporter A. One has the feeling that s/he has just rushed from the dock after interviewing Peter Griffin while the final sentence gives the feeling that the whole nation is waiting to hear this story.

Writing in role serves to extend and enrich dramatic playing in so many ways, including helping to develop a role, revealing more about a person, or providing a different perspective on a dramatic situation. When students write in role, their writing should be used within the drama in some way, so that it is not merely regarded as a writing exercise in itself.

I vividly recall attending a drama workshop several years ago in which we spent some considerable time writing letters in role, and which we then placed on a pile of other letters at the back of the room. The letters were never used in the rest of the session and for all I know were probably thrown away unread even by the workshop instructor.

WRITTEN EVALUATIONS

The final form of writing undertaken by the students is the actual evaluation of the dramatic playing itself, which is later shared by both teacher and students. These evaluations give students an opportunity to reflect on their own participation and learning, and to comment on the dramatic playing itself. In the case of the neighborhood park thematic unit, a simple evaluation form might include a number of sentences to be completed by the class:

THE NEIGHBORHOOD PARK

When I was a planner I learned........................

If we returned to the park a year later, we would find that
....

The best thing about the drama was ....

I think the drama would have been better if ....

Observation

At the beginning of this book, I drew attention to the importance of watching children as they negotiated with one another in dramatic playing or in their spontaneous, social play. Dorothy Heathcote[2] writes that the most developed skill that children bring to school is that of making sense of signs in their immediate environment for their own ends.

I have a child who has a severe language deficit, so I'm only too aware of the ways she has to compensate by learning to read all sorts of signs and signals to enable her to survive in a highly verbal world. Having said that, I know that she has the ability to see something I have often overlooked.

Therefore, although on the surface the skill of observation seems a fundamental and easily acquired skill, I have found it to be extremely complex both to use effectively oneself and to teach to others.

As with questioning and writing, ongoing observation in the dramatic-playing process is not employed solely for the purposes of assessment; observation is also used to extend the learning that is taking place.

There appear to be two major problems concerned with observation in dramatic playing. The first is related to the actual difficulties of trying to understand the meaning of what one is observing. The second one is concerned with finding the language to describe what has been observed. Both problems are directly related to the five areas of learning that have formed the central theme of this book.

For example, there have been many occasions in the dramatic playing sessions I have described where the teacher has deliberately attempted to refine students' powers of observation and their awareness of those powers. The encounter with the elderly woman in the park would be one such instance. However, the dramatic playing session that was most concerned with observation, and finding the language to describe the observations, was the one dealing with the prairie photograph of the family (page 97).

In the first activity the teacher did not ask them to describe what they saw in the picture. Instead, she asked them to talk about the family. Immediately, the students started to make inferences some of which revealed interesting personal insights. For example: "The smaller kid's clothes are too big. He's wearing his brother's old clothes."

Instead of moving directly into the activity in which the class talked to the elder brother, the teacher asked the class to work in small groups and think of questions they would like to ask any member of the family. Again their focus of attention is still on the photograph, but now they have the opportunity to discover the story behind the picture by formulating questions based on their first impression.

As the dramatic playing session proceeds, the teacher is continually refining and extending the students' powers of observation. During the follow-up activities when the students create still images, the teacher continually uses different strategies to draw attention to the meaning that is being conveyed in each image. For example, she asks the class to interpret what they see by creating a caption for one image, and she asks a student in role to step out of another picture and answer questions from the rest of the class.

The slow and thoughtful examination of the still images signals to the class the significance of their work, and the importance of taking time to find the language to describe what they are seeing.

Sometimes students' language focuses directly on the intellectual area of learning, as here: "Although all of the family are affected by the hardships, in a way it seems harder on the mother." (Skill: being aware of similarities and differences).

The focus here is on the emotional area of learning: "The father is remembering how he felt in Spring when he planted the grain." (Skill: recalling past emotions and feelings.)

The focus here is on social learning: "Although the rest of the family wants to leave, the older boy doesn't want to go." (Skill: taking a contrary point of view.)

The focus here is on drama learning: "The kids are closer to their mother than their dad. Look at the way they are kneeling down beside her at the table." (Skill: being aware of space and distance.)

The focus here is on language learning: "Although the dad wants to leave now, he won't be happy in British Columbia. He'll always miss the prairies." (Skill: making predictions.)

In the same way as the teacher helps the students to find the language to discuss what they are seeing, she has to find the language to describe what the students are doing and what they are learning in her anecdotal notes or written summary of the lesson. As I have already indicated throughout the neighborhood park thematic unit, each dramatic playing session focuses on specific areas of learning. Thus in any one activity, the teacher may observe:

Student thinking: Were the students able to demonstrate they could think through a sequence of events in their planning of the park?

Emotional learning: Were all the students able to express their feelings about the section of the park they would be planning?

Social learning: Did the groups organize themselves in such a way everyone could make a contribution to the plan?

Drama learning: Were they able to take a role and work together to sustain one another's belief in the dramatic playing? Language learning: Was the class able to find the descriptive language to create a verbal picture of the park?

A Play Is a Play

At the beginning of this book, students described their perceptions of how drama related to their learning in other areas of the curriculum. The children's words were quoted in an M.A. thesis written by Sabina Harpe,[3] who discusses the different ways in which children view dramatic playing: as a tool, as a web for learning, as a change in teaching approach, and even as a lure to entice children to attend school.

Perhaps the most telling descriptions of dramatic playing come from three students talking about being both within the dramatic playing experience and outside the experience looking in at one and the same time. Here is what they say:

> Sometimes when I'm doing it I wonder how they really were and if this is the way they really acted; if they did that sort of thing.

> I would tell him that it's good for the kids cause it let's them sort of be theirself but be someone else at the same time.

> You just pretend that you're yourself but you're as a different person.

The ability to be engaged in dramatic playing at a feeling level, and yet simultaneously to be sufficiently detached to be able to reflect on that experience, lies at the heart of the dramatic playing experience.

The noted theater and film director, Peter Brook[4], writes:

> In everyday life, "if" is a fiction, in the theatre "if" is an experiment. In everyday life, "if" is an evasion, in the theatre "if" is the truth. When we are persuaded to believe in this truth, then theatre and life are one.
>
> This is a high aim. It sounds like hard work. To play needs much hard work. But when we experience the work as play, then it is not work any more.
>
> A play is a play.

REFERENCES CITED

1. This classification of dramatic playing questions is based on the knowledge framework described in: Mohan, Bernard A. *Language and Content*. Addison-Wesley, 1986.
2. Heathcote, Dorothy. "Signs and Portents." In *Dorothy Heathcote: Collected Writings on Education and Drama*. Edited by Liz Johnson and Cecily O'Neill. Hutchinson, 1984.
3. Harpe, Sabina. *Children's Conceptions of Drama in Education*. M.A. Thesis, University of British Columbia, 1991.
4. Brook, Peter. *The Empty Space*. Macmillan, 1978.

ADDITIONAL READINGS FOR TEACHERS

These books have helped to shape my thinking and teaching. If you wish to learn more about dramatic playing, any one of them will provide you with many insights and helpful suggestions for classroom work.

Barton, Bob, and David Booth. *Stories in the Classroom*. Storytelling, Reading Aloud and Roleplaying with Children. Pembroke, 1990.

Bolton, Gavin. *New Perspectives on Classroom Drama*. Simon and Schuster, 1992.

Byron, Ken. *Drama in the English Classroom*. Routledge, Chapman & Hall, 1986.

Davies, Geoff. *Practical Primary Drama*. Heinemann, 1983.

Morgan, Norah, and Juliana Saxton. *Teaching Drama: A Mind of Many Wonders*. Heinemann, 1987.

Neelands, Jonothan. *Structuring Drama Work*. Cambridge University Press, 1990.

O'Neill, Cecily, et al. *Drama Guidelines*. Heinemann, 1977.

O'Neill, Cecily, and Allan Lambert. *Drama Structures: A Practical Handbook for Teachers*. Stanley Thornes, 1982.

Tarlington, Carole, and Patrick Verriour. *Offstage*. Oxford University Press, 1983.

Tarlington, Carole, and Patrick Verriour. *Role Drama*. Pembroke, 1991.

Wagner, Betty Jane. *Dorothy Heathcote: Drama as a Learning Medium*. National Educational Association, 1976.

ADDITIONAL RESOURCE LIST

For children ages six to nine

All of the following children's illustrated books explore some aspect of the human condition with verve, sensitivity, and insight, and have rich subtexts that could form the basis of dramatic playing:

Andrews, Jan and Ian Wallace. *Very Last First Time.* Douglas and McIntyre, 1990.

Blos, Joan. *Old Henry.* Morrow, 1987.

Bunting, Eve. *The Wall.* Clarion, 1990.

Fox, Mem. *Wilfrid Gordon McDonald Partridge.* Kane Miller, 1985.

Levinson, Riki. *Watch the Stars Come Out.* Dutton, 1985.

Little, Jean, Maggie De Vries and Phoebe Gilman. *Once Upon a Golden Apple.* Viking, 1991.

Mollel, Tololwa, and Paul Morin. *The Orphan Boy.* Oxford University Press, 1990.

Morgan, Allen and Michael Martchenko. *The Magic Hockey Skates.* Oxford University Press, 1991.

Polacco, Patricia. *The Keeping Quilt.* Simon and Schuster, 1988.

Viorst, Judith. *The Tenth Good Thing about Barney.* Atheneum, 1971.

Wallace, Ian. *Chin Chiang and the Dragon's Dance.* Douglas and McIntyre, 1991.

For children ages ten to fourteen

This selection of novels written by contemporary writers explores issues that are of interest and concern to older students, and could form the basis of classroom drama at the intermediate level.

Bawden, Nina. *The Outside Child.* Lothrop, 1989.

Brooks, Bruce. *Everywhere.* Harper, 1990.

Fox, Paula. *The Village by the Sea.* Orchard, 1988.

Garrigue, Sheila. *Between Friends.* Bradbury, 1978.

George, Jean Craighead. *Julie of the Wolves.* Harper, 1972.

Holm, Anne. *North to Freedom.* Harcourt, 1974.

Konigsburg, E.L. *Journey to an 800 Number.* Atheneum, 1982.

Myers, Walter Dean. *Scorpions.* Harper, 1988.

Park, Ruth. *Playing Beatie Bow.* Atheneum, 1982.

Slepian, Jan. *The Broccoli Tapes.* Putnam, 1989.

Southall, Ivan. *Josh.* Macmillan, 1988.

Wrightson, Patricia. *Balyet.* Macmillan, 1989.